BOUNDARYLESS ART

Your Introduction to the Art World

By

Nechama Hermon

Ashley Ludwig

Bethany Miller, Ph.D.

Disclaimer of Liability:

The information provided in this book is for general informational purposes only. While every effort has been made to ensure the accuracy and completeness of the information, the authors and publisher assume no responsibility for errors, omissions, or the suitability of the information for any particular purpose. The authors and publisher shall have no liability for any damages, losses, or injuries arising from the use or reliance upon the information contained in this book.

External Links:

This book may contain references or links to external websites or resources. The inclusion of such references or links does not imply endorsement or recommendation of the content, products, events, or services provided by those external sources. The authors and publisher are not responsible for the availability, accuracy, or reliability of external resources.

Updates and Revisions:

While efforts have been made to ensure the accuracy and relevance of the information contained in this book, it is possible that certain information may become outdated or inaccurate over time. The authors and publisher reserve the right to update, revise, or remove content from this book without prior notice.

By reading this book, you acknowledge that you have read, understood, and agreed to the terms and conditions outlined in this disclaimer.

For permissions or inquiries, please contact: @Boundaryless.Art on Instagram or via our website at boundaryless.art.

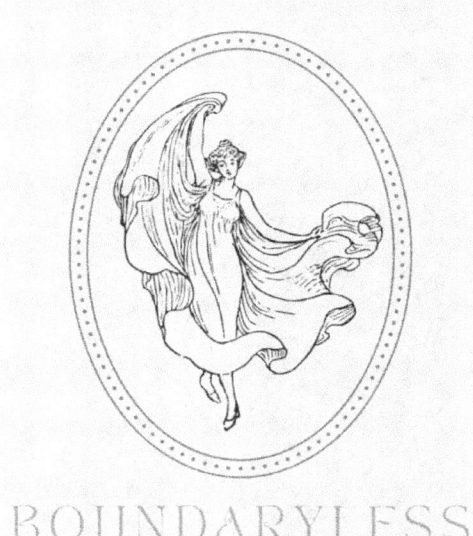

BOUNDARYLESS
.ART

Table of Contents

CHAPTER 5 ✿ Arts & Culture Terms: How to Sound Cool

9

~

Dedication

This book is dedicated to all the knowledge seekers out there that love art like there's nothing else important in this world.

~

Forward ❂ In the Beginning... (And Why Are We Here?)

Arts and culture are essential to the human experience. They provide us with a way to express ourselves, to learn about the world around us, and to connect with others. The arts help us process our experiences (why are we here?) and tackle big hairy philosophical issues. But the aesthetics, oh the beauty, can provide such joy and light in our lives that we may yet find world peace. One can hope!

Art is a powerful tool for communication. It can help us to understand our own emotions, to explore complex ideas, and to share our stories with others. Thus, we create history. Art can also be a form of social commentary, helping us to reflect on the world around us and to challenge the status quo. This creates drama- and that makes things REALLY interesting.

Culture is the shared values, beliefs, and practices of a group of people. It encompasses everything from our food and music to our language and religion. Culture helps to define who we are and gives us a sense of belonging. It also provides us with a framework for understanding the world around us. That's why cultural events are so important to communities.

The arts and culture scene are not just important for individuals, but also for society as a whole. They can help to promote social cohesion, to foster creativity and innovation, and to boost the economy.

In today's increasingly globalized world, arts and culture are more important than ever. They help us to bridge cultural divides, appreciate different perspectives, and build a more tolerant and inclusive society.

We created this book as a valuable resource for anyone who wants to learn more about the importance of the arts and culture. It provides a comprehensive overview of the topic, from the history of art and culture to the latest research on their benefits. The book is also packed with practical tips on how to get involved in the arts and culture in your own community.

Finally, we chose to use Bionic Reading type to facilitate ease of reading and include a resource for many people who read, think, process, or focus differently.

~

CHAPTER 1 ❀ Introduction to Arts and Culture: Everything You Didn't Know You Didn't Know...Or Maybe You Knew It. Whatever. Just Read This.

~

The arts are for everyone. Period.

Whether you're in business, the sciences, management, a creative field, teaching, traveling, or plumbing- no matter if you're a tech bro or a drama queen- even if you're young and carefree or older and slightly more careful, the arts are important for you, us, and everyone. No matter your profession, it's important to embrace cultural activities and understand a bit about art. Why? Glad you asked.

The assertion that the arts are for everyone stands as an immutable truth. Irrespective of one's vocation or avocation, the cultural enrichment derived from engaging with artistic pursuits grants profound benefits across all facets of life. The inescapable essence of art lies in its ability to transcend boundaries, enriching and nourishing the human experience in so many ways. Embracing cultural activities and understanding art helps you tie things together historically, bridges divides, and brings beauty and creativity to our work and lives.

Cultivation of Creativity: Creativity is the lifeblood of progress and innovation. Regardless of the domain, the capacity to think creatively, solve problems, and envision novel possibilities are invaluable traits. Engaging with art nurtures a fertile ground for creativity to flourish, bestowing upon us a wellspring of inspiration and fresh perspectives.

Fostering Empathy and Understanding: Art is a bridge that connects diverse cultures, histories, and experiences. Through art, we immerse ourselves in the narratives of others, cultivating empathy and understanding. In a world fraught with division, this empathetic lens becomes instrumental in fostering harmonious relationships and building a more compassionate society. We like it when you understand and like us! Art helps tell our stories.

Enhancing Communication and Expression: Effective communication is the cornerstone of success in any field. Art, whether visual, performing, or literary, serves as a powerful language that transcends words. By refining our capacity to express and interpret emotions, ideas, and visions, we become more adept communicators, fostering authentic connections with others.

Stimulating Critical Thinking: Art invites us to examine and interpret the complexities of human existence. Analyzing the nuances of an artwork or understanding the layers of meaning in a literary piece sharpens our critical thinking faculties. This acuity in critical analysis serves us well in approaching challenges with clarity and insight.

Nurturing Mental Well-Being: Engaging with the arts offers a sanctuary for introspection and rejuvenation. Whether through the act of creation or immersing oneself in artistic experiences, art has a therapeutic effect on mental well-being, reducing stress, anxiety, and fostering a sense of serenity.

Embodying Cultural Heritage: Art is an embodiment of cultural heritage, a tapestry of traditions handed down through generations. By delving into the arts, we preserve and honor our collective histories, safeguarding the invaluable treasures of our human heritage.

Inspiring Resilience and Adaptability: Art often emerges from the crucible of adversity, reflecting the indomitable spirit of human resilience. Witnessing the triumph of creativity over adversity in art inspires us to cultivate resilience and adaptability in our own lives, navigating challenges with grace and tenacity. It bolsters our "can-do" attitude.

Enhancing Aesthetics in Design and Innovation: The allure of art lies in its aesthetic appeal. By embracing artistic sensibility, professionals in fields ranging from design to technology can charge their creations with elegance, elevating the user experience and fostering lasting connections.

Catalyzing Personal Growth: Art is a vessel through which we explore the depths of our own identities. It reflects who we are. By engaging with art, we embark on a journey of self-discovery and personal growth, uncovering hidden passions, talents, and aspirations that enrich our lives immeasurably.

Fueling a Lifelong Love for Learning: The arts are an infinite realm of exploration. Cultivating an appreciation for art instills a thirst for knowledge and an insatiable curiosity about the world. This love for learning becomes a guiding light, propelling individuals on a lifelong quest for enlightenment.

Basically, the arts constitute an all-encompassing realm, offering myriad gifts to individuals from all walks of life. Got it? Art is a gift. Embracing cultural activities and understanding art is not merely an indulgence but a gateway to a life of enriched experiences, profound insights, and boundless growth. In a world where diversity thrives, the arts stand as a unifying force that celebrates our shared humanity and reminds us of the wonders that await us if we embrace the kaleidoscopic hues of cultural expression.

~

Arts and culture are important for diversity.

The arts, with their myriad forms and manifestations, play a pivotal role in celebrating and promoting diversity. They act as catalysts for cultural progression, welcoming freedom of expression, fostering empathy, appreciating minority artists, resurrecting forgotten art, and encouraging us to embrace our differences. Let's explore how the arts contribute to these fundamental aspects of diversity:

Cultural Progression: Art is an ever-evolving reflection of society. By exploring contemporary art and cultural events, we embrace the progressive evolution of our communities. Artists challenge norms, spark conversations, and push the boundaries of creativity, urging us to question, learn, and adapt as we progress collectively.

Freedom of Expression: Art is a beacon of liberty, allowing individuals from diverse backgrounds to express their stories, perspectives, and emotions. It provides a safe haven for free expression, enabling artists to voice their joys, struggles, and aspirations. In doing so, the arts foster a culture that values open dialogue and respect for varied viewpoints.

Understanding Others: Cultural events and diverse art forms transport us beyond our immediate experiences, offering glimpses into the lives and cultures of others. By witnessing dance, music, theater, and visual arts from different traditions, we develop a deeper understanding of the richness and complexity of the human experience.

Appreciating Minority Artists: Art offers a platform for minority artists to shine and share their unique talents. It enables these creators to celebrate their heritage, enriching the artistic landscape with diverse narratives that resonate with a global audience. Through this appreciation, we foster an inclusive environment that values and uplifts marginalized voices.

Unveiling Forgotten Art from the Past: Art history serves as a treasure trove of forgotten and underrepresented art forms from diverse cultures and civilizations. By unveiling these artworks, we bridge historical gaps and gain insights into the vast tapestry of human creativity, celebrating the contributions of diverse societies throughout history.

Embracing Our Differences: The arts create a space where diversity is not only embraced but celebrated. Dance, theater, literature, and other artistic expressions reflect the beauty of human variation, showcasing the patchwork of identities and experiences that enrich our collective story.

Creating Cultural Dialogue: Festivals and creative performances act as crossroads for cultural exchange. They invite people from diverse backgrounds to come together, fostering meaningful connections and cultivating a sense of unity amidst diversity. These cultural dialogues enrich our perspectives, promoting a more inclusive and compassionate world.

Challenging Stereotypes: Art has the power to challenge preconceived notions and stereotypes, encouraging us to look beyond surface-level assumptions. By engaging with art from different cultures, we break down barriers and cultivate empathy, laying the foundation for a more empathetic and accepting society.

Preserving Indigenous and Traditional Knowledge: Crafts, storytelling, and other indigenous art forms carry the wisdom of ancient cultures. By preserving and supporting these art forms, we honor indigenous knowledge, promoting intergenerational transmission of wisdom and fostering cultural pride.

Building a Unified Identity: Through the arts, we weave the tapestry of our shared humanity. The arts, as well as cultural events, performances, literature, and crafts, enable us to forge connections that transcend borders and cultural divides, ultimately uniting us in our collective quest for beauty, meaning, and understanding.

In essence, the arts are a universal language that transcends barriers and unites us in our diversity. They offer a platform for cultural dialogue, empathy, and celebration, creating an inclusive and compassionate society. By embracing art, we cultivate a world where our differences are celebrated, our stories are heard, and our shared humanity thrives.

~

Art History is long. Here's the short story.

Ah, the epic saga of art through the ages, a colorful canvas of creativity woven by human hands across millennia. Blah blah blah. Let's cut to the good stuff. Here's a whirlwind adventure through time, exploring the earliest known artistic expressions to the grand revolutions of artistic movements, without the final exam. (But if you LIKE final exams (wink), check out our last chapter for the type-A feel-good dopamine hit.)

The Dawn of Art - From Cave Walls to Timeless Treasures: Our artistic voyage begins in prehistoric times, when our ancestors, adorned with creativity, left their mark on cave walls with vivid paintings and handprints. These early artworks, dating back over 40,000 years, were a testament to the human desire to express their world, spirituality, and connection with nature.

The Glorious Ancients - Egypt and Mesopotamia: Fast forward to ancient civilizations like Egypt and Mesopotamia, where art became an exquisite medium to immortalize their beliefs and pharaohs. Behold the awe-inspiring pyramids, colossal statues, and intricate hieroglyphics that stand as testimonies to their architectural and artistic prowess.

Classical Marvels - Greece and Rome: The classical era brought forth the iconic works of Greece and Rome, epitomized by sculptures like the Venus de Milo and the magnificent Parthenon. These masterpieces embodied a profound pursuit of harmony, balance, and idealized human forms.

Medieval Majesty - Illuminated Manuscripts and Cathedrals: As we step into the medieval age, witness the resplendent beauty of illuminated manuscripts adorned with intricate illustrations and gilded accents. Gothic cathedrals soared towards the heavens, displaying stunning stained-glass windows that bathed interiors in an arsenal of colors and divine light.

Renaissance - The Rebirth of Creativity: With the Renaissance came a rebirth of artistic brilliance in Italy, spearheaded by geniuses like Leonardo da Vinci, Michelangelo, and Raphael. Their works, such as the Mona Lisa and the Sistine Chapel ceiling, celebrated humanism, scientific inquiry, and impeccable technique.

Baroque Extravaganza - Drama and Emotion: In the Baroque era, art exuded drama, emotion, and dynamism. Caravaggio's chiaroscuro technique and Rembrandt's captivating self-portraits were among the hallmarks of this period, heightening the sense of realism and emotional intensity in artworks.

Enlightened Enlightenment - Neoclassicism and Romanticism: With the Age of Enlightenment came the Neoclassical movement, harkening back to classical antiquity's idealized forms. Meanwhile, Romanticism embraced emotions, nature, and imagination, as seen in Caspar David Friedrich's evocative landscapes.

Impressionism - Capturing Fleeting Moments: The Impressionists, including Claude Monet and Edgar Degas, dazzled the world with their vibrant brushstrokes, capturing the essence of fleeting moments in natural light. Their revolutionary approach challenged traditional norms, giving birth to modern art.

Cubism - Shattering Perspectives: Picasso and Braque pioneered Cubism, fragmenting reality into geometric shapes, challenging conventional perspectives, and giving birth to abstract art.

Surrealism - Unleashing the Unconscious: Surrealists like Salvador Dalí and René Magritte tapped into the subconscious, blending reality and dreamscapes, birthing haunting and thought-provoking works.

Contemporary Explosion - A Kaleidoscope of Styles: In contemporary times, art exploded into a kaleidoscope of styles and mediums. Pop Art celebrated consumer culture, while abstract expressionists like Jackson Pollock dripped emotions onto the canvas. Digital art and installations pushed the boundaries of artistic possibilities.

And thus, our whirlwind journey through art's vibrant history comes to a close. From the earliest cave paintings to the dazzling diversity of contemporary art, the human spirit has persevered in crafting timeless and transformative creations, transcending time and borders to express the essence of our shared humanity.

~

The future of art is mind boggling. Here's the outrageous story.

As we gaze into the crystal ball of art's future, a mesmerizing panorama of creativity and innovation unfurls before us. The art world is poised for a dynamic transformation, led by cutting-edge technologies, cultural cross-pollination, and a relentless quest for artistic experimentation. Here's a glimpse of what the future of art might hold. Buckle up.

The Digital Art Revolution: Digital art, already a driving force in contemporary art, will continue to expand its frontiers. Advancements in virtual and augmented reality will immerse viewers in interactive art experiences, blurring the boundaries between the real and the virtual. Artists will harness the potential of AI and machine learning to create artworks that respond and adapt to viewers' emotions and reactions, creating personalized artistic encounters.

Crypto Art and Blockchain: The rise of blockchain technology will revolutionize art ownership, provenance, and authenticity. Crypto art, with its unique digital tokens, will empower artists with new monetization models and foster direct connections between creators and collectors. NFTs (Non-Fungible Tokens) will unlock exciting possibilities for artists to tokenize and sell their digital creations, further democratizing the art market.

Space Art Exploration: As humanity ventures further into space, art will accompany this cosmic odyssey. Space artists will capture the celestial wonders and challenges of interplanetary exploration, inspiring us to contemplate our place in the cosmos and the boundaries of human endeavor. Experiments will also produce new art techniques, because someday we'll be writing this from Mars, and we're not sure if we can type so well with those big astronaut gloves on...

Tech Art and Interactivity: Technology will infuse art with interactivity, bridging the gap between spectators and creators. Interactive installations, responsive sculptures, and AI-generated artworks will redefine the traditional art-viewer relationship, making the audience an integral part of the artistic narrative.

Bioart and Sustainability: Artists will increasingly engage with biotechnology, exploring the convergence of art and science. Bioart will raise profound ethical and environmental questions while highlighting the urgency of sustainability. The fusion of living organisms and artistic expression will challenge our perception of art's boundaries.

Global Cultural Fusion: In the future, the art world will witness a fusion of diverse cultural influences, reflecting our interconnected global society. Artists from various backgrounds will collaborate, drawing inspiration from cultural symbiosis, resulting in an exciting tapestry of artistic expressions.

Immersive Media and Art: Virtual galleries and immersive media will redefine how we experience art. Viewers will navigate digital exhibition spaces, teleporting across the globe to explore global art scenes from the comfort of their homes, transcending physical limitations.

Climate Art and Environmental Activism: Climate change and environmental issues will inspire a new wave of art that advocates for change and environmental stewardship. Climate art will use creative expressions to amplify the urgency of safeguarding our planet.

Inclusivity and Representation: The future art world will celebrate and amplify diverse voices, offering greater representation to artists from underrepresented communities. Marginalized narratives will be brought to the forefront, enriching our understanding of human experiences.

Neuroart and Mindscapes: The exploration of brain-computer interfaces and neurotechnology will lead to the emergence of neuroart. Artists will create mind-bending art experiences that interface with the viewer's neural activity, pushing the boundaries of consciousness and perception.

In the ever-evolving landscape of art, the future is boundaryless and brimming with possibilities. As technology and culture converge, artists will continue to be the vanguards of creative exploration, redefining how we perceive, engage, and interact with art. From digital realms to outer space and everything in between, the art world will be a swirl of imagination, provoking thought, inspiring awe, and elevating the human spirit for generations to come. You'll have to be there to experience it.

~

Confront taboos! Arts and culture are a conduit for politics, religion, finance, and other topics we're afraid to discuss in public.

Ah, culture, the enchanting thread that weaves through the tapestry of society, connecting seemingly disparate elements with an irresistible charm. Though often considered taboo in polite conversation, culture serves as an ingenious conduit for exploring a myriad of topics, touching upon politics, religion, sex, money, crime, and more. Let's tiptoe through this cultural garden, keeping it light and non-confrontational. But please, DO discuss at dinner parties. Wink.

Politics - The Dance of Diplomacy: In the realm of politics, culture becomes a masterful diplomat, adept at fostering camaraderie between nations and peoples. Festivals, art exhibitions, and cultural exchanges serve as delightful icebreakers, melting away diplomatic frost and forging bonds of understanding and goodwill. After all, who can resist the allure of cultural delicacies and dance forms that transcend language barriers?

Religion - The Symphony of Spirituality: Religious beliefs, a source of profound inspiration for many, find expression through cultural rituals and traditions. These age-old practices enrich our lives, enveloping us in the harmony of spiritual expression. From colorful festivals to awe-inspiring ceremonies, culture channels the divine in a way that unites hearts and celebrates our shared spiritual journey.

Finance - The Elegance of Economic Expression: Even finance, that realm of numbers and equations, finds an artistic muse in culture. Economic summits and trade shows become vibrant celebrations of commerce, dressed in the hues of cultural exchange. Art auctions and cultural investment forums become captivating performances, where financial expertise meets artistic passion. These events showcase art as a symbol of wealth and prosperity, uniting collectors, investors, and enthusiasts in the artful dance of acquiring cultural treasures. The rhythm of cultural performances harmonizes with the symphony of financial transactions, fostering an environment where numbers are elevated by the poetry of art. Math is a beautiful craft.

Sex - Amour and Angst in Art's Embrace: Art has always been an intimate confidant, capturing love and desire in its many hues. From classical paintings portraying love's tenderness to contemporary artworks celebrating human sensuality, culture encapsulates the complexities of human relationships. With grace and subtlety, art explores the nuances of love and desire, reminding us of the universality of human emotion.

Crime - Capital Capers, Cruelty, and Corruption: In the shadows of culture's gallery, tales of crime occasionally emerge, evoking intrigue and suspense. From art heists depicted in suspenseful films to true stories of art forgery exposed in riveting documentaries, these captivating narratives unravel the enigma of criminal minds and the audacity of art thieves. Even the world of literature delves into crime's mysteries, weaving captivating tales of intrigue and suspense.

Society - Humanity, Habitat, and Happenstance: Culture is a mirror that reflects the soul of society, touching upon sensitive topics with subtlety and grace. Through literature, theater, and film, we contemplate the human condition, pondering questions of morality, justice, and social responsibility. Art acts as a safe space for reflection, offering insights without raising defenses.

Education - A Kaleidoscope of Knowledge: Culture acts as an assemblage of knowledge, enriching education with a myriad of perspectives. Historical reenactments, cultural workshops, and art appreciation classes add hues to the canvas of learning, making education a captivating journey rather than a mundane task.

Environment - The Symphony of Sustainability: In our quest for environmental consciousness, culture emerges as an ally in promoting sustainability. Art installations that weave discarded materials into mesmerizing sculptures and eco-themed festivals awaken our ecological conscience with a gentle nudge, celebrating the beauty of nature and the urgency of conservation.

Innovation - The Confluence of Creativity: Cultural endeavors, such as hackathons with an artistic twist or technology conferences embracing cultural diversity, foster innovation from unexpected angles. By blending art and technology, we discover novel solutions, harnessing the power of creativity to unlock the door to progress.

So, dear friends, let us embrace arts and culture as delightful allies, ushering us into conversations we might shy away from in public. They weave their magic, inviting us to explore, understand, and celebrate the rich tapestry of human experience with or without raising a heated debate. Culture waltzes through the halls of politics, religion, finance, and all spheres of life, turning complex discussions into a graceful symphony that resonates with all hearts.

~

Art scandals, freeports, cultural mysteries, and other things that intrigue us are REALLY what we're here for.

Art Scandals - The Thrills of Deception: Ah, the captivating world of art scandals, where the intoxicating allure of deception and duplicity entangles the art community in a web of intrigue. These tales of audacious forgeries and art heists leave us spellbound, transcending the boundaries of fiction and reality.

The Forger's Brushstroke - Masterpieces in the Shadows: Art forgers, armed with exceptional skill and cunning, test the art world's discernment with meticulously crafted replicas of renowned masterpieces. From Han van Meegeren's counterfeit Vermeers to Elmyr de Hory's fabricated Picassos, these art capers serve as a testament to the forger's brushstroke mirroring the master's hand. While some forgers undertake these acts of deception to expose the vulnerabilities of the art world or challenge its obsession with authenticity, others do so for profit, brazenly slipping forgeries into reputable collections.

Crime and Punishment - The Mystery of the Stolen Masterpieces: The daring theft of iconic artworks from museums and private collections has always stirred our collective imagination. The heist of Edvard Munch's iconic painting "The Scream" in Norway and the audacious "Monet and Renoir" theft from the Museum of Fine Arts in Boston have become the stuff of legend. These daring capers, often involving cunning disguises, ingenious escape routes, and artful subterfuge, captivate us as we root for the safe return of these cultural treasures and marvel at the audacity of the thieves.

Freeports - The Secret Vaults of Treasures: Concealed within bustling cities or nestled discreetly near airports, freeports are enigmatic sanctuaries that house the world's most valuable cultural treasures. These high-security facilities remain veiled in secrecy, holding countless masterpieces and rare artifacts. The labyrinthine halls of freeports, with their temperature-controlled vaults and impenetrable security, have become the stage for thrilling spy novels and Hollywood blockbusters. We can't help but imagine the mysteries that lie behind those guarded doors. Can you say "tax haven"?

Art and Cultural Mysteries - Unraveling Enigmas: In the puzzling world of art and culture, numerous mysteries linger, leaving us with unanswered questions and tantalizing clues. The anonymous identity of the elusive street artist Banksy has become one of the most enduring art mysteries of our time, shrouding the artist's persona in an air of mystique. The sly smile of Leonardo da Vinci's "Mona Lisa" continues to captivate art enthusiasts, sparking endless debates and interpretations. As we contemplate these cultural enigmas, we find ourselves drawn deeper into the art's magnetic allure.

Stolen Art - The Caper of Lost Masterpieces: True tales of art thefts, reminiscent of thrilling Hollywood blockbusters, occasionally unfold in the real world. The audacious theft of iconic artworks, such as Edvard Munch's "The Scream" and Johannes Vermeer's "The Concert," leave us marveling at the art thieves' ingenuity and yearning for the safe return of these lost masterpieces to their rightful homes. The intrigue of these heists and the hunt for stolen art tantalize us, making us curious about the fate of these cultural treasures.

Cultural Repatriation - A Quest for Lost Heritage: The quest to repatriate cultural treasures to their countries of origin is a story of moral conscience and global collaboration. As ancient artifacts find their way back home after years of being housed in foreign collections, these heartwarming stories embody the triumph of cultural heritage and unity. Countries and institutions worldwide work together to return these cultural icons, a reminder of the global effort to preserve our shared past.

Art Mysteries in History - Lost and Found: The annals of art history contain intriguing tales of lost and found masterpieces, where grand artworks vanish, only to resurface after centuries in the unlikeliest of places. The discovery of Vermeer's "The Concert" in a suburban home and the missing panels of the Ghent Altarpiece being found in a Belgian museum attic are among the many art mysteries that tickle our imaginations. These lost-and-found stories rekindle hope that hidden treasures may still be waiting to be discovered.

Lost Art Movements - Fading Footprints of the Past: The annals of art history hold echoes of lost art movements, once thriving and now relegated to the shadows of time. The Futurists, the Symbolists, and the Viennese Secession are just a few examples of artistic revolutions that left indelible footprints but have faded from the spotlight. Exploring these forgotten movements and the unappreciated talents that shaped the course of art sparks our curiosity, prompting us to cherish the hidden gems of history.

Cultural Heritage at Risk - A Race Against Time: As the world undergoes transformation, the fate of cultural heritage hangs in the balance. Climate change, urbanization, and conflict pose existential threats to countless cultural landmarks. Stories of preservation and restoration efforts in the face of these challenges capture our attention, inspiring us to cherish and safeguard our artistic heritage. Efforts to preserve endangered monuments, ancient ruins, and cultural landmarks serve as poignant reminders of our shared responsibility to protect and cherish our cultural legacy.

The dramas of art, from scandals to mysteries, offer an immersive journey through the captivating world of cultural intrigue. As we marvel at the ingenuity of forgers, the secrets hidden within the fortified walls of freeports, and the mysteries that lie within timeless masterpieces, we celebrate the endless allure of art, where every canvas holds a tale waiting to be unveiled. See? Art is cool.

~

Art is an endangered species. Let's talk about art preservation, protecting our cultural heritage, recording art for future generations, and protecting art in dangerous, war-torn, and volatile places.

Art preservation, a noble endeavor that spans the ages, is a vital responsibility. Cultural archaeologists (that's all of us, friends) try to safeguard our cultural heritage and ensure its passage to future generations. As guardians of artistic legacy, we face the crucial task of protecting art from the ravages of time, conflicts, and natural disasters, particularly in volatile or war-torn regions.

Preservation through Conservation - Guardians of Artifacts: Conservationists and art restorers play a pivotal role in preserving art's tangible heritage. With meticulous expertise, they mend fractures, reverse the effects of decay, and breathe new life into aging masterpieces. Through advanced technologies and scientific analysis, they unravel the secrets of artworks, ensuring they endure the test of time.

Digitization - Art Transcending Borders: In the digital age, art transcends borders and connects with global audiences. The digitization of art collections, from paintings and sculptures to ancient artifacts, allows us to record and preserve these treasures for posterity. Online galleries and virtual exhibitions bring art to audiences worldwide, reducing physical vulnerability and promoting wider appreciation.

Cultural Heritage Sites - Sentinels of Time: Cultural heritage sites bear witness to the chapters of human

history. Protecting these landmarks is a testament to our commitment to preserve cultural continuity.
Collaborative efforts by international organizations, local communities, and governments safeguard UNESCO World Heritage Sites, ensuring that their irreplaceable cultural significance remains unscathed.

Protecting Art in Conflict Zones - A Race Against Destruction: Art in war-torn or volatile places faces perilous threats, with looting, vandalism, and destruction looming ominously. Here, the determination to protect artistic heritage shines brighter than ever. Cultural organizations, art historians, and local communities rally to safeguard artifacts and historical sites, rescuing them from the brink of oblivion.

Emergency Response - Art in Crisis: Natural disasters, armed conflicts, and political upheavals call for rapid emergency response to protect vulnerable art collections. Art evacuation plans, emergency shelters, and off-site storage facilities serve as havens, preserving art even in the face of adversity. During turbulent times, valiant efforts by courageous individuals ensure that art survives the chaos.

Community Engagement - The Collective Responsibility: Preserving art goes beyond the efforts of a select few; it's a collective responsibility. Engaging local communities fosters a sense of ownership and pride in their cultural heritage. Through education, workshops, and interactive programs, future generations become the torchbearers of art preservation, safeguarding their heritage with passion and reverence.

Cross-Cultural Collaboration - Bridging Divides: Art knows no borders, and neither should preservation efforts. Cross-cultural collaboration bridges divides, fostering mutual understanding and support. International partnerships bolster art conservation, exchange expertise, and promote peaceful dialogue, highlighting the unifying power of art amidst diversity.

Protecting Street Art - Murals of Urban Expression: Street art, a dynamic form of cultural expression, requires protection in an ever-changing urban landscape. Local governments, art organizations, and communities come together to preserve these ephemeral masterpieces. Initiatives like street art festivals and mural protection programs celebrate urban creativity while ensuring the longevity of these captivating artworks.

Education and Advocacy - Shaping a Resilient Future: Promoting art preservation starts with education and advocacy. Teaching the value of cultural heritage, its importance in shaping identity, and its impact on future generations fosters a culture of preservation and respect. Advocacy initiatives garner public support, urging policymakers to prioritize art protection and ensure its lasting legacy.

As we unite to preserve art, we embrace the essence of our shared humanity, woven through the tapestry of cultures and civilizations. Protecting our cultural heritage and recording art for future generations is a testament to the timelessness of human creativity and the indomitable spirit that seeks to safeguard our collective legacy in the face of challenges and uncertainties. Long live art.

CHAPTER 2 ✿ Quick Art History (Because Really, Who's Got Time?)

~

European Art

Let's journey into the captivating world of European art, where centuries of creativity and innovation have shaped the art scene.

European art encompasses a vast array of styles, movements, and mediums that have evolved over time. From the classical paintings of the Renaissance to the bold experimentation of the Modernists, European art has left an indelible mark on the global artistic landscape.

One of the most iconic art forms in European art is painting. From the breathtaking frescoes of the Sistine Chapel by Michelangelo to the enigmatic masterpieces of Leonardo da Vinci, European painters have produced some of the most celebrated artworks in history. These paintings often depict religious or mythological scenes, portraits of influential figures, landscapes, and still lifes. The meticulous attention to detail, use of light and shadow, and skillful brushwork are hallmark characteristics of European painting.

Sculpture is another prominent art form in Europe. Think of the stunning marble sculptures of ancient Greece and Rome, such as the Venus de Milo and the Discus Thrower. These sculptures showcase the human form in all its grace and power. Throughout European history, sculptors have pushed the boundaries of materials and techniques, creating awe-inspiring works that range from realistic to abstract.

When it comes to famous artworks, it's hard to narrow it down, but a few highlights include the Mona Lisa by Leonardo da Vinci, The Starry Night by Vincent van Gogh, and The Birth of Venus by Sandro Botticelli. These masterpieces have become iconic symbols of European art and have captured the imagination of countless art enthusiasts.

European art has also seen its fair share of famous artists who have shaped the course of art history. Names like Pablo Picasso, Claude Monet, and Salvador Dalí come to mind. These artists, along with many others, have introduced groundbreaking styles and movements that challenged traditional artistic norms. From the Cubist revolution of Picasso to the Impressionist exploration of light and color by Monet, European artists have continuously pushed boundaries, inspiring new generations of creators.

Movements in the European art world have played a significant role in shaping the direction of artistic expression. The Renaissance period, for example, marked a revival of classical ideas and techniques, leading to a surge in scientific exploration and artistic achievements. The Surrealist movement, on the other hand, delved into the realms of the subconscious and dreams, presenting a fantastical and thought-provoking approach to art.

European art is important for numerous reasons. It has not only produced awe-inspiring and timeless masterpieces, but it has also been a driving force behind cultural, social, and political movements. European art has reflected the shifting attitudes and values of societies throughout history, providing glimpses into different eras and worldviews. It has also inspired artists worldwide, serving as a wellspring of creativity and artistic innovation.

So, whether you find yourself captivated by the mysterious smile of the Mona Lisa or moved by the emotional brushstrokes of van Gogh, European art invites you to explore a rich tapestry of creativity, history, and cultural significance. It's a testament to the ingenuity, imagination, and enduring legacy of European artists.

~

Eastern European Art

Let's embark on a journey through the captivating world of Eastern European art, where rich cultural traditions and historical influences have shaped a unique artistic landscape.

Eastern European art encompasses a diverse range of styles, periods, and artistic expressions that have emerged from countries such as Russia, Poland, Ukraine, Hungary, and more. The art from this region reflects a fusion of influences from Western Europe, Byzantine traditions, and indigenous cultural heritage, resulting in a distinctive aesthetic and artistic narrative.

One of the standout art forms in Eastern European art is icon painting. Rooted in the Byzantine tradition, iconography holds a significant place in the religious and cultural life of Eastern European communities. Icons are religious images, typically painted on wood panels, and are characterized by their flat, symbolic style and richly detailed ornamentation. These religious artworks serve as a means of spiritual devotion, storytelling, and cultural identity.

Another prominent art form in Eastern Europe is folk art. Folk artists, often working in rural communities, create vibrant and expressive pieces that reflect the daily lives, beliefs, and traditions of the people. From intricately painted Easter eggs (known as pysanky in Ukraine) to colorful embroidered textiles and wooden carvings, folk art in Eastern Europe is a celebration of heritage and community.

When it comes to famous artworks, there are several notable pieces that showcase the talent and creativity of Eastern European artists. For example, "The Scream" by Edvard Munch, although Norwegian, captures a sense of existential angst that resonates with the experiences of many in Eastern Europe during periods of social and political upheaval. The work of Russian artist Kazimir Malevich, known for his groundbreaking abstract paintings like "Black Square," challenged conventional artistic norms and had a profound impact on the development of modern art.

Eastern European art is also home to a host of renowned artists who have left an indelible mark on the art world. One prominent figure is Wassily Kandinsky, a Russian painter and theorist considered one of the pioneers of abstract art. His innovative use of color and form transformed the way artists approached artistic expression. Another influential artist is Tamara de Lempicka, a Polish painter known for her bold and glamorous Art Deco portraits that epitomized the spirit of the Roaring Twenties.

In terms of art movements, Eastern Europe has witnessed its own unique developments. The Russian Avant-Garde, for example, emerged in the early 20th century and encompassed a wide range of artistic styles, including Cubo-Futurism and Suprematism. These movements embraced experimentation, rejecting traditional forms in favor of abstraction, geometry, and bold use of color.

Eastern European art holds significant importance as it reflects the history, struggles, and resilience of the region's people. It serves as a visual record of cultural identity, political events, and social changes, providing insight into the experiences and aspirations of Eastern European societies. Furthermore, Eastern European art has contributed to the broader artistic discourse, adding diverse perspectives and narratives to the global art scene.

So, whether you find yourself captivated by the intricacies of icon painting, the expressive vitality of folk art, or the innovative spirit of Eastern European artists, the art from this region invites you to explore a rich tapestry of cultural heritage, social commentary, and artistic ingenuity. It's a testament to the power of creativity to transcend borders and tell compelling stories unique to Eastern Europe.

~

Asian Art

Alrighty, let's dive into the vibrant world of Asian art, my friend! Asian art is a captivating tapestry that spans across a multitude of countries and cultures in the massive continent of Asia. We're talking about a vast treasure trove of artistic expressions from places like China, Japan, India, Korea, and many more!

Now, when it comes to types of Asian art, we've got a smorgasbord of styles and mediums to explore. We're talking about beautiful paintings, intricate sculptures, delicate ceramics, dazzling textiles, mesmerizing calligraphy, and even breathtaking architecture. It's like a visual feast that tickles your artistic senses!

Now, let's talk a bit of history. Asian art has a rich heritage that stretches back thousands of years. Ancient Chinese art, for example, dates all the way back to the Neolithic period. The Chinese have been creating amazing artworks for ages, from those iconic terracotta warriors to those delicate porcelain vases you might've seen in museums. They're true masters of craftsmanship!

Speaking of famous artworks, one that definitely deserves a mention is "The Great Wave off Kanagawa" by Katsushika Hokusai. It's a woodblock print from Japan's Edo period, depicting a towering wave crashing down on boats beneath it. It's an absolute icon, instantly recognizable, and has been an inspiration for countless artists worldwide.

When it comes to famous artists, we can't ignore the influential figures like Qi Baishi, a Chinese painter known for his vibrant and lively depictions of nature. His works often feature flowers, birds, and insects, and they're just bursting with energy and joy. Another prominent artist is Raja Ravi Varma, an Indian painter who skillfully blended traditional Indian techniques with European influences, creating stunning portraits and mythological scenes.

Now, let's talk movements! One important movement in Asian art is the Ukiyo-e in Japan, which flourished during the Edo period. Ukiyo-e prints were made using woodblock techniques and were often mass-produced, making art accessible to a broader audience. These prints showcased scenes from daily life, kabuki actors, and beautiful landscapes, capturing the essence of Japanese culture during that time.

So, why is Asian art important? Well, it's not just about admiring the beauty of the artworks themselves. Asian art provides us with a window into the rich and diverse cultures of the continent. It allows us to explore different perspectives, traditions, and aesthetics. It's a testament to the creativity and imagination of the people who lived and created in those times. Plus, it has influenced and continues to inspire artists all over the world, bridging cultures and fostering a global appreciation for artistic expression.

So, my friend, next time you find yourself strolling through an art gallery or museum, make sure to seek out some Asian art. You'll be treated to a captivating journey through history, culture, and the boundless creativity of the human spirit. Enjoy!

~

Pacific Islander Art

Hey there! Let's dive into the colorful world of Pacific Islander art. Get ready for a mix of vibrant paintings, intricate carvings, expressive tattoos, and mind-blowing sculptures!

Pacific Islander art encompasses a wide range of artistic traditions from various island groups, including Polynesia, Melanesia, and Micronesia. Each of these regions has its own unique style and techniques, but they all share a deep connection to their cultural heritage.

One of the standout art forms in Pacific Islander art is the mesmerizing tapa cloth. This is a type of bark cloth made from the inner bark of trees, which is then beaten and painted with intricate designs. Tapa cloths often tell stories, depict important events, or showcase traditional motifs that reflect the cultural identity of the Pacific Island communities.

Another notable art form is wood carving. Pacific Islander artists have mastered the skill of transforming blocks of wood into stunning sculptures. These sculptures can range from small figurines to massive totem poles, each telling tales of legends, ancestral spirits, and the natural world. The level of detail and craftsmanship in these carvings is truly jaw-dropping.

When it comes to famous artworks, there are a few masterpieces that deserve special mention. The Nguzunguzu, a set of ancient stone figures found in the Solomon Islands, are incredible examples of Pacific Islander sculpture. These statues, often depicting ancestral spirits, are characterized by their bold and imposing forms.

In terms of renowned artists, one name that stands out is John Pule from Niue. His paintings are a fusion of traditional Pacific Island motifs with modern styles and themes. Pule's artworks often explore issues of cultural identity, colonialism, and the struggles faced by Pacific Island communities. His use of vibrant colors and powerful imagery make his paintings truly captivating.

In the art world, there has been a growing recognition and appreciation for Pacific Islander art. The influence of Pacific Islander art can be seen in contemporary art movements, where artists draw inspiration from the region's cultural heritage and incorporate it into their work. This fusion of traditional and modern elements creates a unique and thought-provoking artistic expression.

Pacific Islander art is incredibly important because it serves as a visual representation of the rich cultural history and traditions of the Pacific Island communities. Through their art, Pacific Islanders celebrate their ancestral roots, pass down stories and knowledge to future generations, and assert their cultural identity in an ever-changing world. It's a powerful way of preserving and sharing their unique heritage with the rest of the world.

So, next time you come across a stunning Pacific Islander artwork, take a moment to appreciate the intricate details, the vibrant colors, and the deep cultural significance behind it. Pacific Islander art is a true testament to the creativity, resilience, and beauty of the diverse cultures that call the Pacific Islands their home.

~

North America Art

Let's take a trip to explore the diverse and fascinating world of North American art! When we talk about North American art, we're covering a vast region that includes the United States, Canada, Mexico, and the indigenous cultures that have flourished throughout the continent.

North American art encompasses a wide range of artistic styles and mediums. We've got everything from traditional Native American art, which includes breathtaking pottery, intricate beadwork, and powerful totem poles, to contemporary American art that pushes boundaries and challenges conventions. Think paintings, sculptures, photography, installations, and even performance art. There's something for everyone!

Now, let's talk a bit of history. Native American art has a rich heritage that stretches back thousands of years. Each tribe has its unique artistic traditions, symbols, and techniques. For example, the Navajo people are renowned for their stunning rugs and silver jewelry, while the Haida people of the Pacific Northwest create mesmerizing wooden masks and intricate carvings.

When it comes to famous artworks "in" North America, we can't skip over the iconic "Starry Night" by Vincent van Gogh, even though he wasn't North American himself. This masterpiece is housed in the Museum of Modern Art (MoMA) in New York City and has become one of the most recognizable and beloved paintings in the world.

Now, let's talk about some influential artists in North America. One name that should ring a bell is Frida Kahlo, a Mexican artist who lived and worked in the early 20th century. Kahlo's deeply personal and emotive self-portraits, often featuring symbolic elements and surrealistic touches, have made her an icon of self-expression and feminism.

Moving on to American artists, we can't overlook the contributions of Jackson Pollock, a key figure in the Abstract Expressionist movement. Pollock's unique style involved dripping and pouring paint onto canvas, creating dynamic and energetic compositions. His work, such as "No. 5, 1948," challenged traditional notions of painting and paved the way for new artistic possibilities.

Now, in terms of art movements, one significant movement in North America is Pop Art. This movement emerged in the 1950s and '60s, drawing inspiration from popular culture and consumerism. Artists like Andy Warhol and Roy Lichtenstein embraced everyday objects, advertising imagery, and celebrity culture, creating vibrant and bold artworks that reflected the zeitgeist of the time.

Why is North American art important? Well, it's a reflection of the cultural diversity, history, and social dynamics of the region. It allows us to explore and understand the complexities of American and Canadian society, as well as the enduring legacy of indigenous cultures. North American art is a testament to the power of artistic expression in challenging norms, sparking dialogue, and capturing the spirit of a time and place.

So, my friend, next time you find yourself exploring an art gallery or museum in North America, keep your eyes peeled for the stunning works on display. You'll be treated to a journey through diverse perspectives, cultural narratives, and the ever-evolving nature of artistic expression. Enjoy the ride!

~

Central America Art

Here we go now with an artistic adventure through the vibrant world of Central American art! Central American art refers to the artistic traditions and expressions found in the countries that make up the region, including Belize, Costa Rica, El Salvador, Guatemala, Honduras, Nicaragua, and Panama.

Central American art is a colorful tapestry that encompasses a variety of forms and styles. We're talking about intricate indigenous crafts, vibrant paintings, striking sculptures, beautiful textiles, and even architectural wonders. It's a fusion of ancient traditions and contemporary influences, resulting in a visual feast for the senses!

Now, let's delve into the history of Central American art. The region has a rich and diverse cultural heritage that dates back thousands of years. The ancient Maya civilization, for example, left behind a legacy of stunning artwork, including intricate jade carvings, ornate pottery, and magnificent stone monuments depicting gods and rulers. Their art reflects their deep connection to nature, their complex cosmology, and their impressive artistic skills.

Moving on to famous artworks in Central America, one that deserves mention is the "Stone of the Sun" or "Aztec Calendar Stone." Although it's actually from the Aztec civilization, it symbolizes the Mesoamerican cultural connections that spanned across Central America. This massive stone disc, with its intricate carvings representing the Aztec cosmos, is an iconic symbol of the ancient civilizations of the region.

When it comes to prominent artists, Rafael Rodríguez Padilla from Guatemala stands out. His works often reflect the social and political issues faced by the region, using strong symbolism and striking imagery to convey powerful messages. Another notable artist is Francisco Zúñiga from Costa Rica, celebrated for his sculptures that capture the beauty and strength of the human form, often depicting indigenous women.

In terms of art movements, the Muralism movement played a significant role in Central American art. This movement originated in Mexico but had a profound impact on neighboring countries. Artists such as Diego Rivera and David Alfaro Siqueiros utilized large-scale murals to depict historical events, social struggles, and indigenous culture. These murals not only served as works of art but also as political statements and tools for social change.

So, why is Central American art important? It serves as a window into the rich cultural tapestry of the region, preserving and celebrating indigenous traditions, as well as reflecting the complexities of Central American history and identity. Central American art also sheds light on social and political issues, raising awareness and promoting dialogue. It's a testament to the resilience, creativity, and cultural diversity of the people who call this region home.

So, my friend, when you have the chance to explore Central American art, be prepared to immerse yourself in a world of vibrant colors, rich symbolism, and captivating narratives. It's an opportunity to appreciate the beauty and cultural wealth of this often-overlooked region. Enjoy the journey!

~

South America Art

Let's dive deep into an exploration of the captivating realm of South American art! South American art encompasses the artistic expressions found in the diverse countries that make up the continent, including Argentina, Brazil, Colombia, Peru, Chile, and many more.

South American art is a vibrant tapestry that reflects the region's rich cultural heritage and diverse artistic traditions. It encompasses a wide range of mediums and styles, from ancient indigenous art to contemporary installations. We're talking about mesmerizing paintings, intricate textiles, expressive sculptures, dazzling ceramics, and even street art that adorns the walls of bustling cities.

Now, let's delve into the history of South American art. The continent has a long and fascinating artistic legacy, with ancient civilizations like the Inca, Moche, and Nazca leaving behind remarkable artistic treasures. The intricate goldwork of the ancient Incas, the expressive pottery of the Moche, and the mysterious geoglyphs of the Nazca are just a few examples of the artistic marvels that have survived through the ages.

When it comes to famous artworks in South America, one that deserves a mention is "Abaporu" by Tarsila do Amaral from Brazil. This iconic painting is considered one of the most significant works of Latin American modern art. It features a stylized figure with exaggerated proportions and vibrant colors, symbolizing the fusion of indigenous and European influences in Brazilian culture.

Moving on to renowned artists, we can't overlook the contributions of Fernando Botero from Colombia, known for his distinct style featuring voluptuous figures and social satire. Botero's artworks often challenge conventional notions of beauty and provoke thought on societal issues. Another notable figure is Roberto Matta from Chile, an influential surrealist artist whose works explore the depths of the subconscious and cosmic themes.

In terms of art movements, the South American art scene has been shaped by various movements. One influential movement is the Argentinian Concrete Art movement, which emerged in the mid-20th century. Artists like Tomás Maldonado and Alfredo Hlito embraced geometric abstraction and emphasized the purity of form and color, creating visually striking and intellectually rigorous artworks.

Why is South American art important? It serves as a vibrant reflection of the region's cultural diversity, historical narratives, and social realities. South American art embodies the resilience, creativity, and cultural pride of the people who call this continent home. It offers a glimpse into the vibrant tapestry of indigenous traditions, colonial legacies, and contemporary expressions that shape South American identity.

So, my friend, when you have the chance to explore South American art, get ready to be captivated by a kaleidoscope of colors, narratives, and cultural richness. It's an opportunity to celebrate the unique voices and creative visions that emerge from this vibrant continent. Enjoy the adventure!

~

African Art

Now we'll explore the mesmerizing world of African art! African art encompasses the diverse artistic traditions found across the vast and culturally rich continent of Africa, comprising numerous countries, tribes, and societies.

African art is a vibrant tapestry that reflects the continent's deep cultural heritage and artistic diversity. It encompasses a wide range of art forms, including sculpture, painting, mask-making, textiles, pottery, beadwork, and jewelry. Each art form carries its own unique symbolism, aesthetic values, and cultural significance.

Now, let's delve into the history of African art. It has a remarkable lineage that stretches back thousands of years. Ancient African civilizations, such as the Nubians, Egyptians, Benin Kingdom, and Great Zimbabwe, left behind awe-inspiring artistic legacies. From the intricate goldwork of ancient Egypt to the majestic bronze sculptures of the Benin Kingdom, African art showcases the remarkable craftsmanship and creativity of its diverse peoples.

When it comes to famous artworks in African art, one that deserves mention is the exquisite terracotta sculptures of the Nok culture in Nigeria. Dating back over 2,000 years, these sculptures depict human figures with elaborate hairstyles, intricate jewelry, and facial scarification, providing insights into the social and cultural life of ancient African societies.

Moving on to renowned artists, we can't overlook the immense contributions of El Anatsui from Ghana. His mesmerizing sculptures, created from repurposed materials like bottle caps and aluminum, blur the boundaries between sculpture and textile, paying homage to African traditions while engaging with contemporary issues of consumerism and globalization. Another notable figure is Jane Alexander from South Africa, whose thought-provoking installations explore themes of identity, power, and social injustice.

African textiles are a testament to the rich cultural heritage and artistic traditions of the continent. From the intricately woven kente cloth of Ghana to the vibrant and geometric patterns of the wax-printed fabrics found in countries like Nigeria and Senegal, African textiles captivate with their beauty and storytelling. Each textile carries its own unique symbolism, reflecting the diverse cultures and histories of the African people. Skilled artisans employ various techniques such as weaving, dyeing, embroidery, and appliqué to create these stunning works of art. African textiles not only serve as decorative fabrics but also hold deep cultural significance, often being used to mark important ceremonies, celebrate milestones, or convey social status. They are a living expression of African identity, pride, and creativity.

African music is a rhythmic and soulful tapestry that echoes the heartbeat of the continent. It is a vibrant and diverse art form, encompassing a myriad of genres, styles, and instruments. From the infectious rhythms of West African Afrobeat to the melodic chants of traditional South African mbube, African music has a profound ability to move and uplift. It is deeply rooted in community, often serving as a means of storytelling, celebration, and cultural preservation. The continent boasts a wealth of musical talent, from legendary figures like Fela Kuti, Miriam Makeba, and Youssou N'Dour to contemporary artists pushing boundaries and fusing traditional sounds with modern influences. African music resonates with its audiences, transcending language and borders, and serves as a powerful medium for connection, expression, and the celebration of African heritage.

In terms of art movements, one significant movement in African art is the Ndebele wall painting tradition in South Africa. The Ndebele people are known for their vibrant geometric patterns and bold use of color in their wall paintings, which are not only decorative but also carry symbolic meanings, cultural identity, and social messages.

Why is African art important? It serves as a profound expression of Africa's rich cultural heritage, diverse histories, and contemporary experiences. African art challenges stereotypes, celebrates cultural resilience, and gives voice to the narratives, traditions, and struggles of African peoples. Moreover, African art has been a profound influence on modern and contemporary art globally, inspiring artists, collectors, and art enthusiasts alike.

So, my friend, when you have the opportunity to explore African art, get ready to immerse yourself in a world of vibrant colors, intricate patterns, and profound cultural expressions. It's an invitation to appreciate the immense artistic wealth and the profound contributions of Africa to the global art scene. Enjoy the enriching journey!

~

Middle Eastern Art

Let's delve into the enchanting world of Middle Eastern art, a tapestry that weaves together centuries of cultural heritage and artistic expressions. Middle Eastern art encompasses a wide range of diverse styles, mediums, and influences, stemming from countries such as Egypt, Iran, Turkey, Lebanon, and many more.

Middle Eastern art reflects the region's rich historical legacy, religious traditions, and cultural exchanges. It encompasses a variety of art forms, including calligraphy, miniature painting, ceramics, metalwork, carpet weaving, and architectural marvels. Each art form carries its own distinct aesthetic and narrative, showcasing the intricate craftsmanship and profound symbolism deeply embedded in Middle Eastern culture.

When exploring Middle Eastern art history, it is impossible not to mention the mesmerizing beauty of Islamic calligraphy. Calligraphy, often revered as the highest art form in the Islamic world, showcases the mastery of skilled calligraphers who transform Arabic script into elegant and intricate designs. These sacred writings, found in religious texts, architectural elements, and artworks, serve as a visual representation of spirituality and devotion.

Another notable aspect of Middle Eastern art is the rich tradition of miniature painting. This intricate art form emerged during the Persian and Mughal empires and flourished throughout the region. Miniature paintings depict epic tales, historical events, and scenes from daily life with meticulous detail, vibrant colors, and delicate brushwork. These miniature masterpieces offer glimpses into the cultural and social milieu of the time, capturing the essence of Middle Eastern aesthetics.

The intricate blue tilework of the stunning mosques in cities like Isfahan, Iran, and Istanbul, Turkey, cannot be overlooked. These architectural wonders, adorned with geometric patterns, calligraphy, and floral motifs, create a sense of awe and wonder, inviting visitors to marvel at the fusion of art, faith, and architectural grandeur.

Prominent Middle Eastern artists have also made significant contributions to the global art scene. One such figure is Mahmoud Said from Egypt, celebrated for his realistic and evocative paintings that depict Egyptian landscapes, people, and historical events. Another influential artist is Shirin Neshat from Iran, known for her thought-provoking photography and video installations that explore themes of gender, identity, and politics in the Middle Eastern context.

Middle Eastern art has also witnessed the rise of various art movements and contemporary practices. Artists across the region engage with traditional techniques, while also incorporating contemporary concepts, pushing boundaries, and challenging societal norms. These artists use their works as a medium for social commentary, cultural exchange, and self-expression, fostering dialogue and exploring the complexities of the region's diverse identities.

Middle Eastern art holds immense significance as it serves as a visual testament to the region's cultural richness, historical narratives, and spiritual traditions. It provides a window into the artistic achievements, intellectual contributions, and creative resilience of Middle Eastern societies throughout the ages. Moreover, Middle Eastern art encourages cross-cultural understanding, bridging gaps, and fostering appreciation for the region's diverse heritage.

When you have the opportunity to explore Middle Eastern art, be prepared for a world of intricate designs, captivating narratives, and profound cultural expressions. It's an invitation to celebrate the artistic tapestry of the region and gain a deeper understanding of its history, spirituality, and creative genius.

~

CHAPTER 3 ❀ FOMO - What You NEED to Know About Today's Art World

~

Art Tech Trends

Welcome, fellow art enthusiasts, to the enchanting world of the contemporary art scene. Here, innovative technology is orchestrating a symphony of creativity across various artistic disciplines. From music and dance to literature and visual arts, cutting-edge advancements in AI, interactivity, and computer-aided techniques are profoundly influencing artistic expressions.

In the realm of music, AI-generated compositions have emerged as a fascinating new trend. Musicians collaborate with AI algorithms, exploring uncharted melodic territories and blending human emotions with machine precision. The result is a harmonious marriage of classical and avant-garde sounds that captivate our ears and souls alike.

Dance performances have become immersive experiences through interactive technologies. Dancers interact with motion sensors, virtual reality, and augmented reality, shattering the traditional boundaries of the stage. Audiences are no longer passive spectators; they become active participants, traversing realms where the tangible and digital intertwine.

Literature, too, is evolving with AI's literary prowess. Algorithms analyze vast datasets, forging unique narratives and poetic verses. AI-generated literature sparks philosophical debates on authorship, originality, and the essence of creativity itself.

In the visual arts, computer-aided tools empower artists to paint with pixels and sculpt with code. Digital art installations dazzle museums, unraveling surreal worlds where imagination knows no bounds. AI collaborates with artists, assisting and augmenting their visions, leading to awe-inspiring works that push the boundaries of human imagination.

Yet, amidst these technological marvels, the essence of human expression persists. Art remains a reflection of our collective emotions, thoughts, and dreams, regardless of the tools employed. Judging the merits of art today extends beyond the conventional notions of technique and aesthetics. It embraces the fusion of human ingenuity and AI's computational magic.

So, as we embrace this digital Renaissance, let us revel in the interplay of technology and art, where innovation serves as a new brushstroke and interactivity becomes an intrinsic part of the artistic experience. As educated art enthusiasts, we embark on a journey where the future art movements rise on the shoulders of both tradition and technological marvels. Together, we embrace the harmony between art and technology, for it is in this intermingling that the true spirit of creativity finds its everlasting resonance.

~

AR, VR, and Multi-Sensory Art

Step into the awe-inspiring world of Augmented Reality (AR), Virtual Reality (VR), and multi-sensory art—a trinity of transformative technologies that are reshaping the artistic landscape, pushing the boundaries of creative expression, and enchanting audiences worldwide. Let's peek into the unique features, applications, and where to experience these captivating art forms.

Augmented Reality (AR) is an integration of digital content onto the physical world. Artists utilize AR apps or devices like smartphones and tablets to create interactive experiences that blur the line between the real and the virtual. Picture holding up your device in front of the Olympic ruins and seeing images of what the training grounds must have looked like. Whether in museums, galleries, or public spaces, AR art installations breathe life into static pieces. By downloading AR apps like Artivive or Junaio, viewers can unlock hidden dimensions within artworks or sculptures. Interactivity takes center stage, inviting participants to engage with the virtual layers, unveiling captivating narratives and fresh perspectives.

Virtual Reality (VR) offers an unparalleled immersive experience, transporting users to computer-generated environments through VR headsets like Oculus Rift or HTC Vive. In the realm of VR art, artists harness the full potential of three-dimensional space to craft mesmerizing masterpieces. Platforms like Google Tilt Brush provide artists with a virtual canvas to create intricate and breathtaking works of art. Additionally, attendees can virtually witness live performances by their favorite musicians from the front row through apps like MelodyVR, revolutionizing the concert experience.

Multi-sensory art embraces the tactile, olfactory, and auditory dimensions of the human experience, tantalizing all senses. Exhibitions and festivals are the perfect venues to encounter these artworks. Renowned museums like the Tate Modern in London and the Guggenheim in Bilbao occasionally host multi-sensory installations, inviting visitors to explore sculptures with touchable textures, inhale aromatic atmospheres, and experience music interwoven with visual art.

To embark on this enthralling journey, explore art museums and galleries that have embraced AR technology, seek out VR art experiences at technology expos or dedicated VR arcades, and keep an eye out for multi-sensory art events at cultural festivals and immersive exhibitions. Embrace the future of art by delving into these technologies, unearthing the boundless creativity they unlock, and discovering a new dimension of artistic expression. Let your imagination run wild as you partake in this digital renaissance, where art and technology harmonize to create captivating and unforgettable experiences for all art enthusiasts.

~

Street Art

In the bustling heart of urban landscapes, a mesmerizing narrative unfolds upon the city walls. Colors are unchained, and tales unfold upon the buildings themselves. Welcome to the vibrant world of Street Art, where creativity knows no bounds, and the streets themselves become an ever-changing canvas of expression.

There is a different essence in street art because of its diverse creators, its impact on communities, and the spirited dance between legality and rebellion.

The streets come alive with a symphony of colors and shapes, as street art takes center stage in the realm of visual expression. Unbridled by gallery walls, street artists defy conventions and seek to touch the hearts of passersby with every brushstroke. Street art becomes a statement, a poetic response to the city's rhythm, where messages echo, emotions surge, and stories whisper through each mural's intricate details.

To explore the world of street art is to embark on an adventure through the city's alleys and boulevards, for every corner holds the potential to unveil an urban treasure. A quest for a city's hidden art gems unlocks urban treasures. Whether it be the bustling metropolis or a quaint neighborhood, artists have left their mark in every nook and cranny. From the vivid streets of Berlin to the enchanting backstreets of Melbourne, the journey to discover these artistic gems awaits.

The relationship between street art and the law is ever-evolving. In a contemporary renaissance, some cities have embraced street art as an emblem of cultural richness. Designated areas and curated projects now offer legal spaces for artists to showcase their talent freely. This dance between permission and prohibition creates a dynamic backdrop for artistic expression.

Who are the daring souls that breathe life into the city's walls? Street artists are rebel souls and daring spirits. They are an eclectic clan that thrives on creative audacity. From elusive graffiti writers whose identity remains a mystery, to celebrated artists whose fame has transcended the streets, each bears a unique voice. Banksy, the enigmatic maestro of the streets; Shepard Fairey, the propagator of hope; Swoon, the harbinger of humanity – they are just a few of the names that color the vibrant tapestry of street art.

Beyond the surface of vibrant aesthetics, street art weaves a profound social impact. It is a potent catalyst for change, an instrument of empowerment for marginalized voices. It empowers communities and weaves a social tapestry. Artists wield their paint brushes as agents of awareness, painting the city with messages of unity, resistance, and hope. The walls breathe with stories of resilience, urging passersby to pause and reflect on the tapestry of life.

Street art is a journey of endless exploration. It is a realm that transcends borders and surpasses expectations. It is an ever-changing landscape of creativity, where possibilities are boundless. Every stroke, every tag, every mural carries with it the spirit of rebellion, the essence of freedom, and the heartbeat of a generation.

Dear seekers of art and culture, embrace the unchained colors of street art. Roam the cityscape with open eyes and open hearts, for it is in these vibrant streets that art intertwines with life, and creativity dances alongside society. Join the celebration of rebellion and imagination, and let the urban canvas awaken your soul to the enchantment of street art!

~

Artist Residencies

Amidst the bustling digital age, a shimmering oasis awaits the creative souls of young artists. Artist Residencies are a creative odyssey. The secrets of these captivating havens that beckon artists, writers, musicians, and visionaries from all corners of the earth are really a community of growth and artistic encouragement.

Artist residencies scatter across the globe like sparkling stardust, each offering a unique backdrop for artistic musings. They are where an artist finds a temporary home as they develop a particular project, style, or personal growth spurt.

The allure of artist residencies lies not only in their locations but in the extraordinary support they offer. Imagine a world where an artist can unleash their creative spirit without the burden of mundane concerns. Some residencies bestow the gift of financial support by fully funding opportunities, granting stipends, or providing grants to fuel their journey. Creativity becomes the focal point, while needs are tended to by kind patrons.

Diversity reigns supreme in the realm of artist residencies. All artists, no matter their discipline or career stage, find a welcoming embrace within these hallowed grounds. Whether they wield a paintbrush with mastery, weave tales with ink and paper, or conjure melodies from the strings of your heart, an artist's uniqueness is celebrated. Emerging talents dance hand in hand with seasoned maestros, forging a kaleidoscope of artistry that enriches the world.

Artist residencies are gateways to new dimensions of creativity. Destination events and themed residencies invite them to delve into realms unexplored. They collaborate with minds that wander distant horizons, explore themed landscapes, or immerse themselves in unfamiliar cultural realms. These are the crucibles where artistic mettle is honed, and one's spirit is set ablaze with boundless inspiration.

For artists, benevolent forces shine as guiding stars. Foundations and organizations are dedicated to nurturing their dreams and amplifying their voice. Illuminated names like the MacDowell Colony, Yaddo, Delfina Foundation, and others stand resolute, ensuring that the artistic journey is adorned with stardust.

~

The Emergence of Online Art, NFTs, and Digital Arts

In the digital realms that Gen Y and Z call home, a remarkable transformation is underway in the art world. Welcome to the enchanting emergence of Online Art – a realm where pixels dance to create masterpieces, and virtual galleries become the new art sanctuaries. It's a digital Renaissance, and this dynamic shift is captivating the hearts of tech-savvy art enthusiasts.

In the boundless expanse of the internet, a revolutionary art form thrives. Online Art, also known as digital art, transcends traditional boundaries, allowing artists to manifest their creativity through virtual mediums. Through the interplay of code, colors, and pixels, new and mesmerizing artworks are born, breathing life into screens and hearts alike.

Enter the world of Non-Fungible Tokens (NFTs), the magic behind the uniqueness of Online Art. NFTs are digital certificates of authenticity, immutably recorded on blockchain technology. They grant ownership and prove the rarity of a specific digital creation, whether it be a digital painting, a GIF, or a virtual sculpture. With NFTs, artists can forever imbue their digital works with uniqueness, and collectors can truly own a piece of the digital marvel.

Virtual Galleries are a habitat for digital creations. In these ethereal spaces, Online Art finds its home. Art enthusiasts wander through immersive digital landscapes, admiring masterpieces that shimmer with interactivity and movement. These virtual sanctuaries redefine the art-viewing experience, where the audience becomes an active participant in the unfolding narrative of the artwork.

The pioneers of the Digital Renaissance are artists who embrace technology as their paintbrush and code as their canvas. They are tech-forward creators and artists of the digital age. From seasoned digital artists who have embraced the digital realm from the start, to traditional artists who have found new expression in the digital medium, a diverse cohort fuels the resurgence of art in the era of screens and bytes.

As the worlds of art and technology intertwine, a new art market takes shape. Cryptocurrencies, like Ethereum, fuel the economic engine behind NFTs and Online Art. Smart contracts enable artists to receive royalties with every resale, empowering them in ways previously unimagined. This intersection of art and blockchain marks a paradigm shift in how we value, buy, and sell art in the digital age.

Beyond the confines of screens, a virtual universe unfolds with Augmented Reality (AR) and Virtual Reality (VR) art. Through AR, digital art finds a way to inhabit the physical world, blurring the lines between the virtual and reality. VR art becomes an immersive journey, inviting viewers to step into alternate dimensions and experience art like never before.

The emergence of Online Art marks a cultural evolution that bridges generations and redefines creativity. It invites us to rethink what art is, what ownership means, and how we interact with the art world. This digital legacy weaves a narrative of innovation and inclusivity, encouraging everyone to explore their artistic potential in the digital canvas of tomorrow.

~

Interactive Art

In the mesmerizing world of interactive art, artistic experiences transcend the norms and engage both humans and machines. Interactive art installations have ushered in a paradigm shift, offering artists and audiences a dynamic dialogue that leads to both wins and losses.

Wins in interactive art lie in the profound level of engagement and immersion it fosters. By breaking down the barriers between artists and audiences, interactive art blurs the lines of authorship and invites everyone to be a participant, co-creating the experience. This fosters a sense of ownership, making the artwork deeply personal and emotionally resonant. Interactive installations become memorable, leaving a lasting impact on visitors, fostering meaningful connections, and broadening the appeal of contemporary art.

Moreover, interactivity extends beyond human-to-art interaction; artists also explore the harmonious blend of art and artificial intelligence. AI-driven interactive art installations offer limitless possibilities, as machine learning algorithms respond to data inputs, evolving and adapting in real-time. This fusion births artworks that evolve organically, creating a unique experience for each viewer, and posing intriguing questions about the boundaries of creativity and artificial intelligence.

However, there are challenges and losses to be navigated in the realm of interactive art. Striking a balance between the intended artistic vision and the level of audience participation can be delicate. The risk of artworks being reduced to mere novelty or gimmicks, devoid of deeper meaning, is ever-present. Additionally, technical complexities and maintenance of interactive installations can be demanding, requiring ongoing support and updates.

Yet, these challenges fuel the growth and evolution of interactive art. Artists continually push the boundaries, harnessing technology's capabilities to create more profound and authentic experiences. The interplay between computers, AI, and human participation provides fertile ground for innovation, opening doors to uncharted artistic territories.

Therefore, interactive art stands as a testament to the power of collaboration, redefining the relationship between art and audience. Wins arise from the profound engagement, emotional connections, and unique experiences it generates. While losses are encountered in balancing artistic intent and maintaining technical complexities, these challenges inspire growth and evolution. As we navigate this frontier of interactive art, we embrace the fusion of human and machine creativity, shaping a future where the boundaries of artistic expression know no bounds.

~

Neuroart

In a world where science meets imagination, a captivating discovery awaits! Welcome to the enchanting realm of Neuroart, where the wonders of the human mind take shape on canvases and screens alike. Neuroart unveils the secrets of the brain, fusing them with the magical strokes of art. It's all about understanding and representing the human brain's activities, thoughts, and emotions in a visually stunning manner.

Our brains are intricate networks of neurons constantly firing electrical signals and forming connections. These patterns of neural activity reflect our thoughts, feelings, and experiences. Neuroart endeavors to capture these patterns and transform them into beautiful works of art, making the intangible aspects of our consciousness visible.

At the heart of this artistic odyssey lies the extraordinary connection between the brain and the mind. Neuroart creates mesmerizing visual representations that mirror our innermost thoughts, emotions, and subconscious desires. In order to do this, we must step into the laboratory of innovation, where cutting-edge technologies paint the canvas of possibility. Using marvels of science like electroencephalography (EEG) to functional magnetic resonance imaging (fMRI), artists traverse the uncharted terrains of the brain. EEGs record our brain's electrical dance, while fMRI reveals the symphony of blood flow in the regions of thought and creativity. By interpreting this data, artists can understand which areas of the brain are active during specific emotions or actions.

In a unique dance of creativity and science, artists join hands with neuroscientists to unlock the mysteries of the mind. Data from EEGs and fMRIs become art, and art delves deeper into data. In Neuroart, artists often team up with neuroscientists to collect brain activity data while participants engage in various tasks or experience different emotions. These tasks can range from listening to music, solving puzzles, or even meditating. From this artistic alchemy, art emerges! Neuroart takes on myriad forms - stunning paintings, breathtaking sculptures, digital masterpieces, and even virtual reality marvels. Each creation whispers its story, offering a glimpse into the extraordinary symphony of the human mind.

Beyond the strokes of brilliance lies a deeper purpose. Neuroart impacts our understanding of mental health and emotions. Like a guiding light in the labyrinth of feelings, Neuroart unravels the threads of anxiety, depression, and neurodevelopmental conditions, shedding light on the paths to healing and understanding.

If you are dipping your toe in the creative arts, either as an artist or student (or both), embrace your uniqueness and embark on a journey of self-discovery through Neuroart. Unleash your creativity, as you step into the mirror that reflects the essence of who you are, both in conscious thought and the hidden realms of your subconscious. Neuroart aligns perfectly with this exploration and self-discovery. Neuorart is significant for people to discover community and relate to one another, as we can identify how our experiences are captured in the art.

Basically, the canvas of our minds stretches infinitely, and Neuroart invites us to paint it with hues of imagination and innovation. So, dear friends, dare to dream, dare to create, and dare to venture into the unexplored territories of your own mind. If you are interested in creating Neuroart, you can search for EEG and fMRI scans of people doing or experiencing a wide variety of things and use it to inspire your art. For in the boundaryless realm of Neuroart, every stroke reveals a piece of your soul, waiting to be discovered and cherished for eternity.

~

Art Therapy

In the pursuit of healing and self-discovery, art therapy emerges as a profound and transformative practice. We can actually unleash healing through our creativity. In the world of art therapy, we explore art's essence, its practitioners, its benefits, and its origins, offering a glimpse into the therapeutic power of creativity.

Art therapy is a therapeutic approach that utilizes the creative process of art-making to foster emotional, psychological, and mental well-being. It provides a safe and expressive outlet for individuals to communicate, explore, and understand their emotions, thoughts, and experiences through art. Unlike traditional talk therapy, art therapy engages the creative right hemisphere of the brain, allowing for deeper self-exploration and healing.

Art therapy is a versatile modality that can benefit individuals of all ages and backgrounds. It is particularly beneficial for children and adolescents, helping them express feelings they may struggle to articulate verbally. Moreover, it serves as a powerful tool for adults facing various mental health challenges, including depression, anxiety, trauma, and stress-related disorders.

The cost of art therapy can vary depending on factors such as the therapist's qualifications, location, and session duration. In some cases, art therapy may be covered by health insurance plans, making it more accessible to individuals seeking therapeutic support. Additionally, community-based art therapy programs and non-profit organizations may offer more affordable or sliding-scale fee options to accommodate diverse financial circumstances.

Art therapy as a formalized practice has roots dating back to the 1940s. Pioneers like Margaret Naumburg and Edith Kramer played pivotal roles in shaping the field.

Margaret Naumburg, often referred to as the "mother of art therapy," integrated art into psychotherapy as a means of expression and healing. Edith Kramer, another prominent figure, emphasized the importance of the creative process in therapy, considering art as a profound medium for self-discovery and transformation.

Art therapists employ various techniques and modalities to facilitate healing and self-expression. These may include drawing, painting, sculpting, collage-making, and other forms of artistic creation. The focus is not on the artistic quality of the artwork but on the emotional and symbolic content expressed through the creative process.

The therapeutic benefits of art therapy are far-reaching. It can help individuals process and release emotions, reduce stress and anxiety, improve self-esteem and self-awareness, enhance communication skills, and provide a sense of empowerment and agency. Art therapy's nonverbal nature makes it particularly effective for those who find it challenging to articulate their emotions verbally.

Art therapy finds application in various settings, including schools, hospitals, mental health clinics, rehabilitation centers, and community outreach programs. It is a versatile approach that can complement traditional therapeutic interventions or stand alone as an effective form of psychotherapy.

Art therapy stands as a testament to the transformative power of creativity in healing and self-discovery. Through the expressive and nonverbal language of art, individuals can navigate the depths of their emotions, find solace, and embark on a journey of personal growth. As art therapy continues to gain recognition and acceptance, it holds the promise of offering profound healing and empowerment to diverse populations seeking a path to wellness and self-renewal.

~

The Science + Art Movement

The art world is constantly evolving, and the new trends of the 21st century are no exception. In recent years, there has been a growing interest in interactive, innovative, scientific, community-driven, and futuristic arts and cultural movements. These movements are not only contributing to beauty, but they are also having a positive impact on humanity.

One of the most exciting new trends is the science + art movement. This movement brings together artists and scientists to collaborate on projects that explore the intersection of art and science. These projects can take many different forms, from interactive installations to performance art to public art.

For example, the Bioluminescent Night Walk project by the American Museum of Natural History uses bioluminescent bacteria to create a magical nighttime experience. Visitors can walk through a forest of glowing trees and plants, and they can even learn about the science behind bioluminescence.

Another example is the Living Architecture project by the University of Sheffield. This project uses living organisms to create buildings that are self-repairing and energy-efficient. The project is still in its early stages, but it has the potential to revolutionize the way we build and design buildings.

The science + art movement is still in its early stages, but it has the potential to have a profound impact on the world. By bringing together artists and scientists, this movement can help to create new knowledge, new forms of beauty, and a better understanding of the world around us.

In addition to the science + art movement, there are many other new trends in the social sciences and art world that are worth mentioning. These include:

Community-driven art: This type of art is created by and for communities. It often involves collaboration between artists and community members, and it can be used to address social issues or to build community spirit. For example, the Mural Arts Philadelphia program uses art to transform public spaces and to build community. The program has created over 4,000 murals in Philadelphia, and it has helped to reduce crime and to improve the quality of life in the city.

Futuristic art: This type of art explores the future, often using technology and science fiction as inspiration. It can be used to imagine new possibilities for the future, or to warn us about the potential dangers of technology. The Transmediale festival in Berlin showcases new media art that explores the future. The festival has featured work on topics such as artificial intelligence, climate change, and the future of work.

Interactive art: This type of art allows viewers to interact with it in a physical or digital way. This can make art more engaging and immersive, and it can also help to break down the barriers between art and the viewer. The Museum of Broken Relationships in Zagreb, Croatia, is a museum that collects stories of broken relationships. Visitors can interact with the exhibits by sharing their own stories or by listening to the stories of others.

These science and social science trends are all exciting and innovative, and they have the potential to change the way we think about art and our world. They are also helping to make art more accessible and engaging for people of all ages and backgrounds. Most importantly, they are allowing us to see our planet and humanity in new ways that allow us to make positive changes for our future.

~

The Global Film Industry

The world of cinema is a mesmerizing realm where creativity knows no bounds, and imaginations come to life on silver screens. As we venture into the captivating global film industry, we uncover the powerhouse nations, mind-boggling financial figures, and intriguing facts that have shaped the magic of cinema for lovers of the storytelling and cinematic arts.

At the heart of the film industry stands Hollywood, the iconic Tinseltown that embodies the very essence of cinematic brilliance. The famed "Hollywood" sign, initially created as a real estate advertisement, has since become an immortal symbol of American filmmaking and global stardom. In 1911, Hollywood's Nestor Film Company established the world's first movie studio, igniting a journey that would forever shape the course of cinema.

In a journey across continents, we find ourselves captivated by Bollywood, India's cinematic splendor. Boasting over 1,000 films produced annually, Bollywood holds the record for the largest film output globally. Stepping back to 1913, we witness the birth of Indian cinema with the premiere of "Raja Harishchandra," a pioneering moment that laid the foundation for Bollywood's illustrious storytelling tradition.

China's cinematic revolution unfolds before our eyes as we explore its staggering rise in the global film industry. With the world's largest film market by box office revenue, China's film industry has embraced both domestic and international audiences, igniting a new era of cinematic influence. We delve into the strict regulations on foreign films, uncovering their role in shaping China's cinematic journey.

Amidst the glitz of Hollywood's and Bollywood's grandeur, the European art house cinema gracefully weaves its own spell. At the Cannes Film Festival, a beacon of artistic excellence, we celebrate independent productions that dazzle with unique storytelling and thought-provoking narratives. Europe's charm lies in its embrace of creativity, cultivating a cinematic tapestry that captivates the soul.

Crossing continents to Africa, we discover Nollywood's radiant gem. As the second-largest film industry in terms of film output, Nollywood's prolific productions have captured hearts far and wide. Witnessing the birth of the term "Nollywood" and Nigeria's artistic fervor, we find a cinematic treasure that shines with untamed brilliance.

Delving into the dazzling world of box office triumphs, we witness how films like "Avatar" and the Marvel Cinematic Universe have redefined the concept of blockbuster success. "Avatar," the highest-grossing film of all time, showcases the global appeal of cinematic masterpieces, while the MCU's unparalleled success has created an interwoven tapestry of storytelling like never before.

Entering the glittering stage of the Academy Awards, we witness the celebration of cinematic excellence since 1929. The Oscars honor outstanding performances and remarkable filmmaking, serving as a global platform that recognizes talent and artistic achievement. Immersed in the glitz and glamor, we discover the indelible impact the Oscars leave on the film industry.

As we peek behind the curtain, we find technology as the driving force behind cinema's evolution. From the groundbreaking CGI of "Jurassic Park" to Alfonso Cuarón's awe-inspiring "Gravity," technological innovations have elevated cinematic experiences to unprecedented heights, enthralling audiences and expanding the realms of storytelling.

Finally, let us celebrate the power of diverse storytelling and the rise of inclusive voices in the film industry. "Black Panther" and "Parasite" exemplify films that have shattered boundaries and ignited a movement toward greater representation. As the world embraces these cinematic dreams, they awaken to the boundless possibilities that cinema holds, forever inspiring new generations to share their stories within the silver screens of the world.

In the enthralling world of cinema, there are tales that captivate, inspire, and transport us to unimaginable realms. From Hollywood's glimmering stars to Bollywood's vibrant dance numbers, from China's cinematic rise to Nollywood's African splendor, the global film industry unites us all with its enchanting magic. As Generations Y and X embrace these cinematic dreams, they awaken to the unlimited possibilities that cinema holds, forever igniting their own stories within the silver screens of the world.

~

Breaking Records

In the music industry, certain artists have mastered the art of breaking records and achieving unparalleled success with their tours. Now we explore the common factors that set these tours apart, enabling them to amass staggering profits while others may struggle to make a mark.

Artists who achieve record-breaking success possess a global fan base and mass appeal that transcends boundaries. Their music resonates with diverse audiences, crossing genres and languages, and forging a universal connection with listeners worldwide. This widespread appeal attracts a massive following and ensures sold-out shows wherever they perform.

The success of record-breaking tours often lies in the artists' iconic branding and authenticity. These artists have carefully cultivated their public images, staying true to their artistic vision while also evolving over time. Their authenticity creates a genuine connection with fans, inspiring loyalty and driving ticket sales.

Record-breaking tours are not merely concerts; they are grand spectacles and immersive experiences. These tours feature elaborate stage designs, state-of-the-art technology, mesmerizing visuals, and stunning choreography. The meticulous attention to production value ensures fans are treated to unforgettable and awe-inspiring performances.

Artists who achieve record-breaking success are unafraid of artistic evolution. They continuously push boundaries, experiment with new sounds, and reinvent themselves creatively. This willingness to evolve keeps their music fresh and exciting, appealing to both longtime fans and new audiences.

Successful tours are backed by strategic marketing and promotion campaigns. From targeted social media campaigns to exclusive fan experiences, these artists and their teams leave no stone unturned to generate buzz and excitement around their tours. Their marketing prowess ensures tickets sell out rapidly.

The artists who break records often embrace inclusivity and empowerment. Their music carries messages that resonate with diverse audiences, addressing social issues and promoting positive change. By connecting with fans on a deeper level and championing important causes, they create a sense of community around their tours.

Artists who achieve record-breaking success prioritize fan engagement and interaction. They use digital platforms to connect directly with their supporters, offering behind-the-scenes glimpses, exclusive content, and surprise interactions. This engagement fosters a strong and devoted fan base, generating excitement around their tours.

Above all, record-breaking tours are defined by unforgettable live performances. These artists deliver electrifying and emotionally charged shows that leave audiences in awe. Their ability to command the stage, captivate the audience, and leave a lasting impression ensures their tours are celebrated as unforgettable musical experiences.

The success of record-breaking tours in the music industry stems from a combination of factors. Global stardom, mass appeal, iconic branding, authenticity, strategic marketing, and inclusivity play pivotal roles in attracting fervent fans and elevating these tours to cultural phenomena. Moreover, the willingness to experiment and evolve creatively, along with unforgettable live performances, cements the artists' status as tour de force in the music world. These common elements define the winning formula that sets apart record-breaking tours from the rest, ensuring their place in music history as milestones of artistic achievement and commercial triumph.

~

Who is Buying Expensive Art...and Why?

There are some crazy expensive artworks out there. Absolutely lavish art treasures are being bought and sold every day. The buyers of expensive art primarily consist of wealthy individuals, including business magnates, celebrities, high-net-worth investors, and art enthusiasts. Their motivations for buying expensive art can vary, but common reasons include: investment diversification, status and prestige, personal passion and aesthetics, support for artists and cultural institutions, emotional and intellectual stimulation, and an appreciation for history and culture.

What is the allure of big-ticket art? Is it purely an investment or something more profound?

Expensive art purchases often have both financial and emotional motivations. While some buyers view art as a valuable investment asset with potential for appreciation, many are genuinely passionate about art, finding emotional fulfillment and intellectual stimulation in the pieces they acquire. But art is also the marketplace of dreams.

Expensive art is bought and sold through various channels, including renowned auction houses such as Christie's and Sotheby's, prestigious art galleries, private sales, art fairs, and online art platforms.

Art can be considered an alternative investment, but it comes with unique risks and considerations. While some artworks have demonstrated impressive appreciation over time, the art market can be volatile and less liquid compared to traditional financial investments.

The amount collectors invest in expensive art varies widely, from tens of thousands to millions or even hundreds of millions of dollars per artwork. The returns on art investments can also vary significantly, with some pieces appreciating substantially over time, while others may not yield significant financial gains.

Historically, the art world has been perceived as an exclusive realm accessible only to the wealthy and well-connected. However, efforts are being made to democratize art and make it more inclusive. Online platforms, art fairs, and emerging artist initiatives are broadening access to art and encouraging a wider range of participants.

~

Freeports and Other Sexy Scandals

Shadows and scandals unveiling the dark side of the art world. In the dazzling world of Arts & Culture, where creativity knows no bounds, there also lurks an underside. Let's venture into the mysterious realm of freeports and other scandals that have cast shadows over the art world.

The enigmatic world of freeports is a news darling. Hidden from the public eye, freeports are secured storage facilities where valuable art and other assets can be stored with tax advantages and limited oversight. We delve into the history and purpose of freeports, understanding how they have become a sanctuary for art owned by the wealthy elite.

Freeports are the art market's secret vault. They have become hubs for art transactions beyond the reach of tax authorities and regulatory scrutiny. There are many controversies surrounding these private storage zones and their potential role in facilitating illegal activities.

Freeports are designated areas where goods can be imported, stored, processed, and re-exported without paying customs duties or taxes. The first freeport was established in the 12th century in the Italian city of Livorno. Freeports were later established in other parts of Europe, as well as in the United States and other countries.

In recent years, there has been a renewed interest in freeports, as governments have looked for ways to boost economic growth and create jobs. In the United Kingdom, for example, the government has announced plans to create 10 new freeports.

Some of the most famous freeports in the world include:

-- Freeport of Hong Kong: This is one of the largest and most successful freeports in the world. It is located in the Special Administrative Region of Hong Kong, China.

-- Freeport of Singapore: This is another major freeport located in Asia. It is located in the Republic of Singapore.

-- Freeport of Dubai: This is a large freeport located in the United Arab Emirates. It is known for its role in the global trade of commodities.

-- **Freeport of Hamburg:** This is a major freeport located in Germany. It is known for its role in the global trade of automobiles.

Freeports have become increasingly popular with the art world in recent years. This is because freeports offer a number of advantages for art collectors and dealers. For example, art can be stored in a freeport without paying customs duties or taxes. This can save collectors a significant amount of money.

In addition, freeports offer a secure environment for storing art. Facilities include optimal environments for art storage, not to mention privacy. The security measures in freeports are often very tight, which helps to protect art from theft and damage.

If you are interested in storing your art in a freeport, there are a few things you need to do. First, you need to find a freeport that is willing to accept art storage. Not all freeports allow art to be stored on their premises.

Once you have found a freeport that is willing to accept art storage, you will need to contact them to discuss the terms and conditions of storage. The terms and conditions will vary from freeport to freeport, so it is important to read them carefully before you agree to anything.

The rules for storing art in a freeport vary from freeport to freeport. However, there are some general rules that apply to all freeports. For example, art that is stored in a freeport must be properly insured. In addition, the art must be properly documented.

It is also important to note that art that is stored in a freeport cannot be sold or exhibited without paying customs duties and taxes. This is why freeports are often used by collectors who want to store art for the long term.

Freeports are always a controversial topic, but they can offer a number of benefits to businesses and individuals. They can help to boost economic growth, create jobs, and provide a secure environment for storing valuable goods. However, it is important to be aware of the rules and regulations that apply to freeports before you decide to use one.

~

Controversies in the Art World

-- In the seemingly serene world of art, controversies can lurk beneath the surface, challenging norms, provoking debates, and igniting passionate discussions. Let's delve into the various controversies that have shaken the art world, revealing the complexities and tensions that exist within this captivating realm.

-- Artistic Expression vs. Offense: One of the most significant controversies revolves around the clash between artistic expression and offense. Art has the power to push boundaries, challenge societal norms, and provoke thought. However, some works of art have faced criticism for being deemed offensive or disrespectful, sparking debates over the limits of creative freedom and the impact of art on sensitive topics.

-- **Authenticity and Forgeries:** The art world has not been immune to forgery scandals, where unscrupulous individuals create counterfeit artworks to deceive collectors and art enthusiasts. The discovery of a fake masterpiece can not only have financial repercussions but also raise questions about the credibility of art authentication processes and the preservation of artistic legacies.

-- **Cultural Appropriation:** In an increasingly interconnected world, art has faced scrutiny for cultural appropriation, where artists from one culture borrow elements from another without proper acknowledgment or understanding of their significance. This raises concerns about respecting cultural heritage, intellectual property, and the responsibility of artists to represent diverse cultures accurately.

-- **Art as Investment or Commodity:** As art values escalate, the perception of art as a lucrative investment opportunity has grown. This has led to the commodification of art, where some artworks are seen more as financial assets than expressions of creativity and culture. The commercialization of art has sparked debates about its impact on artistic integrity and the exclusion of aspiring artists from the market.

-- **Ownership and Restitution of Cultural Artifacts:** The ownership and restitution of cultural artifacts have been contentious issues, with many museums and private collections housing artworks with disputed origins. Calls for the repatriation of cultural treasures to their countries of origin have raised questions about colonial histories, ethical responsibilities, and the rightful ownership of cultural heritage.

-- Censorship and Freedom of Expression: The art world
has grappled with issues of censorship and freedom of
expression, where certain artworks have faced
suppression due to their controversial themes or
political statements. This raises questions about the role
of artistic institutions, the responsibility of curators, and
the implications of limiting creative expression.

-- Gender Representation and Artistic Canon:
Historically, female artists have faced discrimination and
marginalization in the art world, resulting in an
underrepresentation of their works in museums and art
history textbooks. The controversy surrounding gender
representation has spurred movements to reevaluate the
artistic canon and amplify the voices of female artists
and artists from marginalized communities.

-- Ethics of Art Sales and Auctions: The high-stakes
world of art sales and auctions has faced controversies
regarding transparency, undisclosed conflicts of
interest, and inflated prices. The ethical considerations
of art transactions have been questioned, prompting
discussions about fairness, accountability, and the role
of intermediaries in the art market.

-- The Stolen Art Trail: Intrigue awaits on a thrilling
journey through the world of art theft. From famous
heists to looted artifacts, the stories of lost masterpieces
and the tireless efforts to recover and repatriate stolen
art to their rightful homes is a constant battle.

-- Forgeries and Fakes - The Art of Deception: The art
world is not immune to deception. Unmasking the
counterfeiters and forgers is a full-time job. The
intriguing tales of fake artworks that manage to infiltrate

the market are consistent across fashion and other creative industries. Understanding the challenges faced by experts in authenticating and preserving the integrity of art proves how daunting this task is.

-- Money Laundering: The Dark Canvas: Behind the beauty of art lies an intricate web of financial transactions. The murky waters of money laundering are where art has been used as a conduit to conceal illicit funds and evade detection. It's imperative to combat this growing menace.

-- Cultural Heritage in Peril: In the pursuit of valuable artifacts, cultural heritage faces the threat of destruction and exploitation. There are controversial practices of art trafficking and illegal excavation which contribute to the loss and destruction of priceless treasures from ancient civilizations.

-- The Art World's Ethics - Navigating Gray Areas: As we confront these scandals, we address the ethical considerations within the art world. Delve into the complexities of balancing art commerce with preserving cultural heritage and ensuring transparency and accountability with care.

Illuminating the path forward involves shining a light on the efforts to address and rectify the dark corners of the art world. From international agreements to increased due diligence, we must explore the measures taken to safeguard the integrity of art and protect its place in our shared human heritage.

We have uncovered many hidden facets of the art world, reminding ourselves of the importance of safeguarding culture, preserving authenticity, and holding the sanctity of art in the highest regard. As we explore the shadows and scandals, we encourage art enthusiasts to be discerning observers of the art world's brilliance and its shadows.

Controversies in the art world are a testament to the dynamic and multifaceted nature of artistic expression. From debates over creative freedom to issues of cultural sensitivity, the art world continuously grapples with complexities and tensions. Embracing these controversies with open dialogue and critical reflection is crucial for the growth and evolution of art, ensuring that it remains a vibrant and transformative force in society.

~

CHAPTER 4 ✿ Getting Your Culture On: What to Expect When You're Expecting...to Go Someplace Cultural

~

Go to a Museum

Museums are all the rage. They have history, or art, or science, or hands-on experiences, and more. Here's what you can expect when you visit a museum:

1. Admission and Tickets: Museums typically have an admission fee, although some museums offer free entry or have special discounted days or hours. It's advisable to check the museum's website or contact them in advance to inquire about ticket prices, any discounts available, and whether tickets can be purchased online or at the museum.

2. Opening Hours: Museums have specific opening hours, which can vary from one museum to another. It's important to check the museum's schedule to plan your visit accordingly. Some museums may have extended hours on certain days or be closed on specific dates, so it's best to verify the opening hours before you go.

3. Visitor Information and Maps: Most museums have visitor information desks or centers near the entrance. These areas provide maps, brochures, and other resources that can help you navigate the museum and make the most of your visit. Staff members at these desks are often available to answer questions and

provide guidance about the museum's exhibits and facilities.

4. Collections and Exhibitions: Museums house various collections of artworks, historical artifacts, scientific specimens, and cultural objects. These collections can cover a wide range of topics, such as art, history, science, natural history, or specific cultural themes. Museums often organize temporary or special exhibitions alongside their permanent collections, offering unique and curated displays that focus on specific themes, artists, or periods.

5. Information and Interpretation: Museums typically provide information about the exhibits and artworks on display. This can be in the form of wall labels or interactive displays placed near each exhibit, providing details about the object's history, context, and significance. Audio guides, multimedia presentations, or guided tours may also be available to offer deeper insights into the collections.

6. Etiquette and Rules: When visiting a museum, it's important to observe certain etiquette and rules to ensure a respectful and pleasant experience for everyone. This often includes refraining from touching the artworks or artifacts unless explicitly allowed, following any photography restrictions, maintaining a quiet demeanor, and respecting any designated paths or barriers.

7. Museum Shops and Cafés: Many museums have shops or gift stores where you can purchase books, replicas, souvenirs, or art-related merchandise related to the museum's collections. Some museums also have

cafés or restaurants where you can take a break, grab a snack, or enjoy a meal during your visit. These amenities can add to your overall museum experience.

8. Interactive or Hands-on Exhibits: Some museums, especially those focused on science, children, or specific themes, offer interactive or hands-on exhibits. These exhibits encourage visitor participation and provide a more engaging and interactive experience. They are particularly enjoyable for families or those looking for a more immersive museum visit.

9. Special Events and Programs: Museums often organize special events, lectures, workshops, or educational programs related to their collections or temporary exhibitions. These events may provide opportunities to learn more about specific topics, interact with experts, or engage in hands-on activities. Checking the museum's calendar or website can help you discover any upcoming events that might interest you.

Visiting a museum offers a chance to explore and appreciate human history, art, culture, and scientific discoveries. Take your time, immerse yourself in the exhibits, and enjoy the educational and enriching experience of a museum visit!

~

Go to the Opera

Going to the opera is a fabulous experience. You need the 411 about what happens before the curtain goes up:

1. Getting Tickets: You can usually purchase opera tickets online through the official website of the opera house or theater. Alternatively, you can visit the box office in person to buy tickets. Prices for opera tickets can vary depending on factors such as seating location, production scale, and the specific opera company. It's best to check the opera house's website or contact them directly for ticket pricing information.

2. Dress Code: Attending the opera is often considered a special occasion, so dressing formally or semi-formally is customary. Men often wear suits or dress shirts with slacks, while women opt for elegant dresses or dressy separates. However, the dress code can vary depending on the venue and the specific production, so it's a good idea to check if there are any specific guidelines mentioned on the opera house's website.

3. Performance Duration: Opera performances can vary in length, but they generally last between two to four hours, including intermissions. More elaborate productions or those with multiple acts might be longer, so it's worth checking the specific opera's runtime in advance.

4. Intermissions: Most operas have intermissions, usually lasting around 15 to 30 minutes. This gives the audience an opportunity to stretch their legs, visit restrooms, and socialize. You can also pre-order drinks or snacks for the intermission, which leads us to the next point.

5. Food and Drinks: Many opera houses have bars or concession stands where you can purchase drinks and light refreshments before the performance and during intermissions. However, the availability of food and drinks can vary, so it's advisable to check beforehand or bring your own water bottle or snacks.

6. Temperature in the Theater: Opera theaters are often kept slightly cooler than room temperature to ensure the comfort of the performers and prevent the audience from feeling too warm. It's a good idea to dress in layers or bring a light sweater or jacket in case you feel chilly during the performance.

7. Language: Operas are typically performed in the language they were composed in, such as Italian, German, French, or English, depending on the production. However, most opera houses provide supertitles or subtitles projected above the stage or on individual screens, translating the lyrics into the language of the audience. This allows you to follow the storyline and understand the dialogue even if you're not familiar with the language.

8. Program: Opera houses usually provide programs or playbills that include information about the specific opera, the performers, and the production team. These programs are often available for purchase or included with your ticket. They can enhance your understanding and enjoyment of the performance by providing context, synopses, and other relevant information.

9. Opera Performance: Operas are typically divided into acts, with each act containing several scenes. The performance takes place on a stage, accompanied by an orchestra situated in a designated area, usually below or in front of the stage. The performers, including the singers (vocalists), chorus, and sometimes dancers,

convey the story through a combination of singing, acting, and sometimes dancing. The orchestra provides the musical accompaniment, and there may also be elaborate sets, costumes, and lighting to enhance the visual experience.

During the opera, it's important to be respectful of the performers and other audience members by refraining from talking or using electronic devices. Applause and standing ovations are customary at the end of each act and at the conclusion of the performance to show appreciation for the performers.

Attending the opera can be a memorable and enriching experience, combining beautiful music, captivating storytelling, and impressive stagecraft. Enjoy the performance and immerse yourself in the world of opera!

~

Visit an Art Gallery

Art Galleries are the coolest thing in the art world. You need to go. Here's what you can generally expect when you visit an art gallery:

1. **Admission and Tickets:** Art galleries often have an admission fee, but some galleries offer free entry, particularly for certain exhibitions or specific days of the week. It's a good idea to check the gallery's website or contact them in advance to inquire about ticket prices and any special offers.

2. **Dress Code:** Unlike the opera, art galleries generally have a more relaxed dress code. Casual attire is

typically acceptable, but it's always a good idea to dress comfortably, especially if you plan to spend a significant amount of time exploring the gallery. Except, of course, if the gallery is hosting a special event. In that case, dress the part. Chic, badass, or stylish- be ready to mingle.

3. Artwork on Display: Art galleries showcase a variety of artworks, including paintings, sculptures, installations, photographs, and more. Each gallery often has its own collection or hosts temporary exhibitions featuring works by specific artists or art movements. It's a great opportunity to view diverse artistic styles, themes, and mediums.

4. Duration of Visit: The length of your visit to an art gallery is entirely up to you. Some people may spend a few hours exploring the entire gallery, while others might prefer a shorter visit focusing on specific exhibits or artworks of interest. You can take your time to appreciate the art at your own pace.

5. Information and Interpretation: Art galleries often provide information about the exhibited artworks, either through wall labels placed near each piece or through brochures or audio guides available at the entrance. These resources can provide details about the artist, the artwork's title, medium, and sometimes insights into the artistic process or historical context. They can enrich your understanding and appreciation of the art.

6. Silence and Etiquette: Art galleries are typically quiet spaces where visitors can engage with the artwork in a contemplative atmosphere. It's customary to maintain a quiet and respectful demeanor, refraining from talking

loudly or using mobile devices with sound. This allows everyone to immerse themselves in the art and enjoy a tranquil environment.

7. Photography: Many galleries have specific policies regarding photography. Some may allow photography without flash, while others may prohibit it entirely to protect the artworks. It's important to check with the gallery staff or signage to understand the photography guidelines and respect the artist's rights and the gallery's policies.

8. Gallery Shop and Café: Larger art galleries often have a shop where you can purchase art-related merchandise, books, prints, or souvenirs. Some galleries also have cafés or restaurants where you can take a break, have a snack, or enjoy a beverage. These amenities can enhance your overall gallery experience.

9. Guided Tours and Events: Some art galleries offer guided tours led by knowledgeable staff or curators who provide insights and interpretation of the artworks. Additionally, galleries may organize special events, such as artist talks, panel discussions, workshops, or performances. Checking the gallery's schedule or website can help you discover any upcoming events that might interest you.

Visiting an art gallery provides an opportunity to engage with visual arts, explore different perspectives, and discover new artists. It's a chance to appreciate creativity and expand your horizons. Enjoy your visit and immerse yourself in the world of art!

~

Visit a Historical Site

There's nothing cooler than seeing history in person. Up close. You know, at the place where it all happened. Here's what to know for the next time you visit a historical site:

1. Admission and Tickets: Historical sites often have an admission fee or ticketing system to enter. The ticket prices can vary depending on factors such as the significance of the site, its maintenance costs, and whether it's a public or private site. Some sites also offer discounts for students, seniors, or local residents. It's advisable to check the website or contact the site in advance for ticket information and any special requirements.

2. Opening Hours: Historical sites typically have specific opening hours. It's important to check the operating schedule in advance to plan your visit accordingly. Some sites may have seasonal variations in their hours or even be closed on certain days, so it's good to confirm the site's availability before you go.

3. Visitor Center and Information: Many historical sites have visitor centers or information desks near the entrance. These centers provide valuable resources such as maps, brochures, audio guides, and knowledgeable staff who can offer insights into the site's history, significance, and notable features. Take advantage of these resources to enhance your understanding and make the most of your visit.

4. Guided Tours: Some historical sites offer guided tours led by experts or trained guides. These tours provide

detailed information, stories, and historical context about the site, enhancing your understanding and appreciation of its significance. Guided tours may be available at specific times or require prior reservation, so it's worth checking the site's offerings in advance.

5. Historical Significance: Historical sites often have cultural, architectural, or archaeological importance. They may have witnessed significant events, served as the residence of notable figures, or contain artifacts of historical value. Researching the site beforehand or utilizing provided information can help you appreciate its historical context and significance.

6. Walking and Exploring: Historical sites often involve walking or exploring the grounds to fully appreciate their features. This may include architectural structures, ruins, preserved buildings, gardens, or archaeological remains. Wear comfortable shoes and be prepared for uneven terrain or stairs, especially in older sites. If you're not up for significant physical activity, be sure to check how accommodating the site is. Not all places have elevators or full accessibility, unfortunately. Boo.

7. Interpretive Displays and Exhibits: Some historical sites have interpretive displays or exhibits that provide additional information about the site's history, artifacts, or cultural context. These displays may be housed in on-site museums or visitor centers. Take the time to explore these exhibits to gain a deeper understanding of the site's historical significance.

8. Respect and Preservation: When visiting a historical site, it's important to respect its integrity and preservation. Follow any posted rules or guidelines,

such as not touching artifacts or structures, avoiding restricted areas, and refraining from littering. You can't sit on every ancient stone pillar or walk on antique floor mosaics. Respecting the site helps ensure its preservation for future generations.

9. Photography: Many historical sites allow photography for personal use. However, some sites may have restrictions or require permits for professional photography, commercial use, or the use of tripods. Sometimes you can't use a flash. Check the site's photography policy and abide by any guidelines to respect the site's rules and the rights of others.

Visiting a historical site offers an opportunity to step back in time, connect with the past, and appreciate the cultural heritage. It allows you to explore and learn from tangible reminders of history. Enjoy your visit and immerse yourself in the rich narratives of the past!

~

Visit a Theater for a Live Performance

Live performances in a theater are the best! From plays to drama to dance and more, here's what you can generally expect when you visit a theater:

1. Booking Tickets: To attend a live performance at a theater, you will need to book tickets in advance. Tickets can usually be purchased online through the theater's official website or through authorized ticketing platforms. Depending on the popularity of the performance and the theater, tickets may sell out quickly, so it's advisable to book well in advance.

2. Ticket Pricing: Ticket prices for live **performances** at theaters can vary depending on factors such as the production, seating location, and the reputation of the theater. The theater's website or box office will provide information about ticket prices, discounts for students or seniors, and any special offers available. Some places, like TKTS in New York City, have discount tickets for same-day performances.

3. Dress Code: The dress code for theater performances can vary depending on the theater and the specific performance. Some theaters have a formal dress code, where dressing up in attire such as suits, dresses, or cocktail attire is customary. Other theaters may have a more relaxed dress code, allowing for casual or smart-casual clothing. It's a good idea to check the theater's website or contact them for any specific dress code guidelines.

4. Performance Duration: Live theater performances can have varying durations depending on the production. Plays can range from one to three hours, while musicals may be longer due to additional songs and choreography. The theater's website or the ticketing platform usually provides an estimated duration for the performance, allowing you to plan your evening accordingly.

5. Arrival Time: It's advisable to arrive at the theater at least 15 to 30 minutes before the scheduled start time of the performance. This gives you enough time to find your seat, visit restrooms if needed, and settle in before the show begins. Some theaters may have specific guidelines regarding latecomers, so it's best to be punctual. There's usually some cool music going on beforehand to get you in the mood. And if you're not sitting on the aisle seat, you'll have to "excuse me, excuse me, excuse me…" all the way to your seat. You'll want to do this well before the curtain rises.

6. Intermission: Many theater performances have an intermission, typically lasting around 10 to 20 minutes. This break allows the audience to stretch their legs, visit restrooms, or purchase refreshments from the theater's concessions. It's a good opportunity to relax and discuss the performance with your companions.

7. Food and Drinks: Theaters often have concessions or bars where you can purchase drinks and snacks before the performance and during intermissions. However, not all theaters allow food and drinks inside the auditorium, so it's important to check the specific policies of the theater you're attending. Some theaters may offer pre-show dining options, allowing you to have a meal before the performance. Prices at the concession stand are usually much higher than your usual mini-market, so be prepared to shell out some cash or tap pay without looking shocked.

8. Theater Etiquette: When attending a live performance, it's important to observe theater etiquette. This includes turning off or silencing your mobile devices, refraining from talking during the performance, and avoiding any disruptive behavior that could disturb the performers or fellow audience members. Even the softest whispers to your friends are disturbing to those around you. Photography and recording are generally not allowed during the performance unless explicitly permitted.

9. Programs: Many theaters provide programs or playbills that contain information about the performance, the cast and crew, and background details about the production. Larger programs and books about the theater or show are often available for purchase at the theater, and they can enhance your understanding and enjoyment of the performance by providing context and insights. Save your playbill as a great (free) souvenir.

Live theater performances offer a unique and immersive experience, bringing stories to life on stage. Enjoy the show, appreciate the talent of the performers, and immerse yourself in the captivating world of live theater!

~

Go to a Vegas Show

Remember, what happens in Vegas stays in Vegas (wink)! Las Vegas is a sexy kind of place with a million shows for everyone of every age, style, and discernment. From funny to magical to flashy (literally) to acrobatic to musical and beyond, there really is something for everyone. Here's what to know about seeing a show in Las Vegas:

1. Show Selection and Tickets: Las Vegas is known for its wide variety of shows, including magic shows, musical performances, acrobatics, comedy acts, and more. Start by selecting the show you want to see and check the availability of tickets. Tickets can be purchased online through official ticketing platforms, the show's website, or at the box office of the respective venue.

2. Ticket Pricing: Show ticket prices in Las Vegas can vary depending on factors such as the popularity of the performer or production, seating location, and the venue. Prices can range from affordable to quite expensive, depending on your preferences and budget. It's advisable to check the ticket prices in advance and compare options to find the best fit for you. And yes, check those tourist booklets in your hotel room for some discounts here and there.

3. Show Venues: Las Vegas has numerous theaters and show venues, often located within hotels and resorts along the famous Las Vegas Strip. Each venue has its own unique atmosphere and seating arrangement, so it's a good idea to familiarize yourself with the venue's layout before you go. Check the venue's website for details on directions, parking, and any specific guidelines or policies. Note to the wise: Vegas venues are absolutely ginormous. Huge, we say, huge! Arrive early and figure out where you're going. This may mean walking through a casino and asking for directions within the location, because most are in mega-size buildings that are hotel-casino-theater-shopping-dining venues all in one. There will be a lot of walking.

4. Showtimes and Duration: Las Vegas shows typically have multiple performances scheduled throughout the week, offering flexibility in choosing a showtime that suits your schedule. Show durations can vary, but most performances last around 90 minutes to 2 hours, including any intermissions. Check the show's website or ticketing platform for the exact showtimes and duration.

5. Dress Code: The dress code for Las Vegas shows varies depending on the type of show and the venue. Some shows may have a formal dress code, requiring cocktail attire or formal wear, while others have a more relaxed dress code allowing for casual or smart-casual clothing. It's best to check the specific show's dress code recommendations to ensure you are appropriately dressed. Pro tip: many people flaunt it in Las Vegas. Wear your sequins and punk makeup any time, any place.

6. Theater Etiquette: When attending a show in Las Vegas, it's important to observe theater etiquette. This includes arriving on time, switching off mobile devices, refraining from talking during the performance, and avoiding any behavior that could distract the performers or other audience members. Respect the rules and guidelines of the venue to ensure a pleasant experience for everyone. But at the end, yell and applaud wildly. They love that.

7. Pre-Show Dining and Drinks: Many Las Vegas show venues have restaurants or bars within the premises, allowing you to have a meal or enjoy pre-show drinks before the performance. It's a good idea to make reservations if you plan to dine before the show, as popular restaurants can fill up quickly. Check the venue's website for dining options and availability. Again, leave yourself extra time. Just because a restaurant or bar is in the same venue, it might actually be a 15 minute walk away.

8. Entertainment Complexes: Some Las Vegas hotels and resorts have entertainment complexes that offer a range of shows and performances. These complexes often include multiple theaters or performance spaces, along with other amenities such as casinos, nightclubs, and dining options. Exploring these complexes can provide a diverse range of entertainment choices for your visit. These venues are not only enormous, they are decorated in crazy styles! Ranging from opulent and elegant to themed-out cartoon land, the Vegas casinos and hotels are spectacular exhibits themselves. Take extra time to take photos in the fabulous settings.

9. Show Experience: Las Vegas shows are renowned for their high production values, impressive stage setups, and talented performers. Sit back, relax, and immerse yourself in the spectacle of the show. From captivating performances to stunning visual effects, Las Vegas shows aim to provide an unforgettable experience for the audience. Soak in the vibrant energy of Las Vegas entertainment!

~

Go to Cirque du Soleil

Acrobatics, storytelling, and amazement, anyone? If you're up for a performance that will boggle your mind and challenge your notion of what acrobats and dancers and storytellers and costume creators can do, Cirque du Soleil is for you. Here's what to expect when you go to see a Cirque du Soleil show:

1. Show Selection and Tickets: Cirque du Soleil is renowned for its spectacular acrobatic performances and artistic displays. Start by selecting the Cirque du Soleil show you want to see, as they have different shows with their own unique themes and storylines. Tickets can be

purchased online through the official Cirque du Soleil website or through authorized ticketing platforms. All the seats offer a unique perspective, and the performers often wander through the audience, so do not be afraid of sitting somewhere new. There are no bad seats.

2. Ticket Pricing: Cirque du Soleil ticket prices can vary depending on factors such as the popularity of the show, seating location, and the venue. Prices can range from affordable to more expensive, depending on the seating category and the demand for the specific show. It's advisable to check the ticket prices in advance and compare options to find the best fit for your budget.

3. Show Venues: Cirque du Soleil shows are held in various locations around the world, including permanent theaters in Las Vegas and touring productions in different cities. Each venue has its own unique atmosphere and seating arrangement. When booking tickets, make sure to check the specific venue and its location. Inside the venue, the decorations will be fantastic, and they help to tell the story of the performance. The lights change, the walls come alive, the props are used by the performers, hoops and fabric hang from the ceiling, and many things are larger than life. The sets are a special kind of wonderful.

4. Showtimes and Duration: Cirque du Soleil shows typically have multiple performances scheduled throughout the week. Show durations can vary, but most performances last around 90 minutes to 2 hours, including any intermissions. It's recommended to check the show's official website or ticketing platform for the exact showtimes and duration.

5. **Dress Code:** Cirque du Soleil shows generally do not have a specific dress code, so you can dress comfortably and according to your preference. Casual or smart-casual attire is suitable for most shows. However, you may want to consider the venue's atmosphere and dress slightly more formal if you're attending a show in a prestigious theater. And if you're a queen, feel free to dress and wear makeup with flair.

6. **Theater Etiquette:** When attending a Cirque du Soleil show, it's important to observe theater etiquette. This includes arriving on time, switching off mobile devices, refraining from talking during the performance, and avoiding any behavior that could distract the performers or other audience members. You won't have time to socialize anyway- you'll be looking everywhere so as not to miss a single thing during the performance.

7. **Pre-Show Dining and Drinks:** Some Cirque du Soleil shows may offer pre-show dining experiences or have restaurants and bars within the venue. This gives you the opportunity to have a meal or enjoy drinks before the show. Check the show's official website or contact the venue to inquire about any dining options available.

8. **Unique Performance:** Cirque du Soleil shows are known for their incredible acrobatics, stunning visual effects, and captivating storytelling. Prepare to be amazed by the skills and talents of the performers as they take you on a journey through breathtaking acts and artistic presentations. Be ready to witness a one-of-a-kind performance that combines acrobatics, music, dance, and theatrical elements.

9. Souvenirs and Merchandise: Cirque du Soleil shows usually have merchandise booths or shops where you can purchase show-related souvenirs, apparel, and other memorabilia. This gives you the opportunity to bring home a piece of the Cirque du Soleil experience and cherish the memories of the show.

Attending a Cirque du Soleil show promises an extraordinary blend of artistry, athleticism, and creativity. Enjoy the mesmerizing performances, immerse yourself in the enchanting world of Cirque du Soleil, and create lasting memories of this unique live entertainment experience.

~

Attend a Music Festival

Music is the language of love, of life, and of our generation! It becomes larger than life when you attend a music festival. Feel your favorite vibes in the open air, with longer performances, with mixed combinations of artists, and with surprising guest performances. You've got to be there to live it. Here's what you can expect when attending a music festival:

1. Festival Selection and Tickets: Music festivals come in various genres and sizes, catering to different musical tastes. Start by selecting the music festival you want to attend and check its official website or authorized ticketing platforms for ticket availability. Festival tickets are usually sold in different tiers or packages, offering various options for entry. There's usually a selection of tickets that don't have a seat- sometimes you bring your own chair or blanket, sometimes you stand in the mosh pit or along the edges or in the waaaaaay back, and sometimes you're in folding chairs or stadium seating. Be aware of what you're buying.

2. Ticket Pricing: Music festival ticket prices can vary depending on factors such as the popularity of the festival, the lineup of artists, and the type of ticket you choose (e.g., general admission, VIP, single-day pass, or multi-day pass). Prices can range from affordable to more expensive, depending on the festival's reputation and offerings.

3. Festival Dates and Location: Music festivals typically take place over one or more days, often in outdoor venues or dedicated festival grounds. Check the festival's website or official announcements for the specific dates and location. It's important to consider factors such as transportation, accommodation, and weather conditions when planning your festival visit.

4. Lineup and Schedule: Music festivals feature multiple artists and bands performing on different stages throughout the event. Familiarize yourself with the festival lineup and schedule to plan which artists you want to see and when they are performing. Festival websites or mobile apps usually provide detailed schedules to help you make the most of your experience.

5. Festival Facilities: Music festivals often provide various facilities to enhance the attendee experience. These may include food vendors, bars, restrooms, medical tents, merchandise stands, and designated areas for relaxation or socializing. Familiarize yourself with the festival map and available facilities to make the

most of your time at the event. Know ahead of time whether you can bring your dog, bring food, bring a bag, bring umbrellas, etc. There may be metal detectors at the entrance or a security and safety tent to pass by.

6. Festival Attire and Essentials: Festival attire is often casual and comfortable, allowing you to enjoy the music and move freely. Consider the weather conditions and dress accordingly, with layers for cooler temperatures or sun protection for outdoor festivals. Don't forget essentials like sunscreen, a hat, sunglasses, comfortable footwear, and a small backpack or bag to carry your belongings, if allowed.

7. Festival Etiquette and Safety: Respect for fellow festival goers and safety are crucial at music festivals. Follow any guidelines or rules set by the festival organizers, including restrictions on prohibited items, behavior, or drug and alcohol policies. Stay hydrated, be mindful of your personal belongings, and take care of yourself and those around you. And if you're going to party, party safely. Look out for your friends. We love you and we care.

8. Performance Experience: Music festivals offer a unique and energetic atmosphere, with multiple artists performing back-to-back on different stages. Explore the festival grounds, discover new music, and enjoy the performances that resonate with you. It's common for attendees to move between stages or areas, so plan your schedule accordingly to catch your favorite acts.

9. Festival Community and Vibes: Music festivals are known for creating a sense of community and shared experiences. Interact with fellow festival goers, embrace

the positive vibes, and immerse yourself in the collective excitement. Engage in activities offered by the festival, such as art installations, workshops, or interactive experiences, to make the most of your festival visit.

Attending a music festival allows you to immerse yourself in a diverse range of musical acts, connect with like-minded individuals, and create lasting memories. Embrace the festival spirit, enjoy the music, and celebrate the joy of live performances in a vibrant and energetic atmosphere.

~

Attend a Comedy Show

You are hilarious! And if you're not, you can go to a comedy show to hear other hilarious people. Here's what you can generally expect when attending a comedy show:

1. Show Selection and Tickets: Comedy shows feature various comedians, each with their own unique style and humor. Start by selecting the comedy show or comedian you want to see and check the availability of tickets. Tickets can often be purchased online through official ticketing platforms, the comedian's website, or at the venue's box office.

2. Ticket Pricing: Comedy show ticket prices can vary depending on factors such as the popularity of the comedian, the venue, and the seating location. Prices can range from affordable to more expensive, depending on the demand for the show. It's advisable to check

ticket prices in advance and compare options to find the best fit for your budget.

3. Show Venue: Comedy shows are typically held in comedy clubs, theaters, or dedicated venues. Each venue may have its own unique atmosphere, seating arrangement, and capacity. Familiarize yourself with the venue's location, parking options, and any specific guidelines or policies they may have.

4. Showtime and Duration: Comedy shows usually have specific showtimes, so it's important to check the show's schedule in advance. Show durations can vary, but most comedy shows last around 60 to 90 minutes, depending on the comedian and the format of the show. Some shows may have an opening act or a warm-up comedian before the main performance.

5. Dress Code: Comedy shows typically have a casual dress code. You can dress comfortably in casual or smart-casual attire. There is no strict requirement, but it's recommended to avoid wearing clothing that may distract the performer or other audience members. And if you wear something outrageous, you may be singled out by the comedian for a laugh mid-show.

6. Theater Etiquette: When attending a comedy show, it's important to observe theater etiquette. This includes arriving on time, switching off mobile devices or setting them to silent mode, refraining from talking during the performance, and avoiding any behavior that could distract the comedian or other audience members. Respecting the rules and guidelines of the venue ensures a pleasant experience for everyone.

7. **Drinks and Refreshments:** Many comedy venues have bars or concessions where you can purchase drinks and refreshments before or during the show. It's common to enjoy a drink or two during a comedy show, but be mindful not to overindulge and disturb the performance or fellow audience members. Some venues include a 1-drink or 2-drink minimum in the entry price. This doesn't have to be an alcoholic drink, it's just a way for the venue to make more money. So be a good guest, buy that bottle of water or drink of choice and support the venue and performers.

8. **Interaction and Audience Participation:** Comedy shows often involve interaction and audience participation. Comedians may engage with the audience, tell jokes based on audience responses, or invite volunteers on stage. If you're comfortable with participating, embrace the opportunity to be part of the show's interactive elements. If you're not comfortable with participating, don't sit in the front row. Pro tip!

9. **Laughter and Enjoyment:** The primary goal of attending a comedy show is to have a good time and enjoy the humor. Sit back, relax, and let the comedian entertain you with their jokes, stories, and comedic timing. Laughter is encouraged, so don't be afraid to laugh out loud and join in the collective enjoyment of the performance. And be forewarned, some jokes may be off color, sexual in nature, or offensive to certain audiences. It's wise to Google the performers beforehand if you're concerned about this.

Attending a comedy show offers a chance to unwind, laugh, and enjoy the comedic talents of the performers. Embrace the humor, appreciate the comedic artistry, and savor the experience of live comedy in a relaxed and entertaining environment.

~

Attend the Ballet

One of the most beautiful arts is the ballet! It's not just a dance, it's a story and a performance and a musical experience. Here's what you can generally expect when attending a ballet performance:

1. Ballet Selection and Tickets: Ballet performances feature classical and contemporary dance pieces. Start by selecting the ballet performance you want to see and check the availability of tickets. Tickets can be purchased online through official ticketing platforms, the ballet company's website, or at the venue's box office.

2. Ticket Pricing: Ballet ticket prices can vary depending on factors such as the reputation of the ballet company, the production's popularity, and the seating location. Prices can range from affordable to more expensive, depending on the demand for the performance and the venue. It's advisable to check ticket prices in advance and compare options to find the best fit for your budget.

3. Venue and Seating: Ballet performances are held in theaters or opera houses, often with specific seating arrangements. Familiarize yourself with the venue's location, seating chart, and any specific guidelines or policies they may have. Consider choosing seats that provide a good view of the stage and allow you to fully appreciate the dancers' movements.

4. Showtime and Duration: Ballet performances have specific showtimes, so it's important to check the performance schedule in advance. Ballets typically consist of multiple acts and last around two to three hours, including intermissions. The duration may vary depending on the production and the inclusion of any additional elements.

5. Dress Code: Ballet performances often have a formal or semi-formal dress code. It's recommended to dress elegantly, such as wearing cocktail attire or formal wear. Men may opt for suits or dress shirts with trousers, while women can choose dresses, skirts, or dressy pantsuits. Dressing appropriately adds to the overall experience and respect for the art form.

6. Theater Etiquette: When attending a ballet performance, it's important to observe proper theater etiquette. Arrive on time, switch off mobile devices, and avoid talking during the performance. Refrain from taking photos or recording videos, as it can be disruptive and disrespectful to the performers and other audience members.

7. Intermissions and Refreshments: Ballet performances often have intermissions, allowing you to take a break and stretch your legs. Some venues have refreshment areas or bars where you can purchase drinks or light snacks. Take advantage of the intermission to relax, socialize, and appreciate the ambiance of the theater.

8. Language and Storytelling: Ballet performances often tell stories through dance, without spoken dialogue. The narrative is conveyed through the dancers' movements, expressions, and the accompanying music. While

understanding the language of the performance is not necessary, familiarizing yourself with the story or plot beforehand can enhance your appreciation of the ballet.

9. Performance Experience: Watching a ballet performance is a visually stunning experience. Immerse yourself in the grace, precision, and artistry of the dancers as they bring the choreography to life. Pay attention to the dancers' technique, their storytelling through movements, and the synchronization with the music. Allow yourself to be captivated by the beauty and expressiveness of the ballet.

Attending a ballet performance offers a unique opportunity to witness the beauty and precision of dance. Embrace the elegance, enjoy the performances, and let yourself be transported into a world of artistry and storytelling through the grace and skill of the ballet dancers.

~

CHAPTER 5 ✿ Arts & Culture Terms: How to Sound Cool

~

Abstract

Abstract art is a style of visual art that does not attempt to represent an accurate depiction of visual reality. Instead, it uses shapes, colors, forms, and marks to achieve its effect. In abstract art, the artist may choose to focus on the expressive qualities of the artwork rather than its representational aspects. This style of art often emphasizes the emotional or spiritual dimensions of the artist's experience, allowing for an interpretation up to the viewer.

Abstract art is important to arts and culture for several reasons. Firstly, it challenges traditional notions of representation and pushes the boundaries of artistic expression. By breaking away from the constraints of realism, abstract art opens up new possibilities for creativity and innovation. It encourages artists to explore their own unique visions and experiment with different techniques and materials. Additionally, abstract art invites viewers to engage with the artwork on a more personal and introspective level. It allows for individual interpretation and encourages a deeper exploration of one's own emotions and perceptions. This can lead to a greater appreciation and understanding of the complexities of human experience, fostering empathy and connection within society.

~

Abrasion

Abrasion is a term used to describe the process of wearing away or scraping off the surface of an object or material through friction or contact with another object. In the context of arts and culture, abrasion can play a significant role in various artistic practices. For instance, in sculpture, artists may intentionally use abrasion techniques to create texture or to reveal underlying layers of the material. This can add depth and visual interest to the artwork, as well as evoke a sense of history or transformation.

In addition, abrasion can also be important in the conservation and restoration of artworks. Over time, artworks can become damaged or deteriorated, and abrasion techniques can be employed to carefully remove dirt, grime, or unwanted layers of paint without causing further harm. This process helps to preserve the integrity and aesthetic value of the artwork, allowing future generations to appreciate and study it. Overall, abrasion serves as a valuable tool in the artistic process and the preservation of cultural heritage.

~

Action painting

Action painting, also known as gestural abstraction, is a style of painting that emphasizes the physical act of creating art. It's like a dynamic and expressive dance between the artist and the canvas. Action painting is characterized by spontaneous brushstrokes, drips, splatters, and energetic movements, capturing the raw and immediate emotions of the artist in the artwork.

Action painting holds significant importance in arts and culture as it challenges traditional techniques and focuses on the process of creating art rather than a predetermined outcome. It celebrates the freedom, energy, and spontaneity of artistic expression. Action painting invites viewers to witness the artist's passion, movement, and connection to the artwork.

By embracing this style, artists break free from conventions, allowing emotions and instincts to guide their creative journey. Action painting often captures the intensity and vitality of the human experience, reflecting the artist's state of mind in the artwork. It encourages viewers to engage actively with the artwork, interpreting the energetic brushstrokes and exploring the layers of texture and color. By understanding and appreciating action painting, we celebrate the power of artistic expression and the diversity of creative approaches within our culture. Action painting challenges us to embrace spontaneity, liberation, and personal expression in both art and life.

~

Aesthetic

Aesthetic, in the realm of art, refers to the overall visual or sensory experience and the subjective perception of beauty, harmony, and emotional impact that an artwork elicits. It's like the unique essence and quality that makes an artwork visually appealing and evokes a particular mood or response.

An aesthetic shapes our emotional and intellectual connection to art. It influences our preferences, interpretations, and appreciation of artistic expressions across various mediums and styles.

Aesthetic considerations encompass elements such as color, composition, texture, form, and concept, which combine to create a cohesive and engaging artistic experience. Artists carefully craft aesthetics to communicate their ideas, convey emotions, challenge societal norms, or inspire contemplation. Understanding and appreciating aesthetics allows us to explore different artistic perspectives, broaden our understanding of beauty, and develop a critical eye for artistic quality.

Aesthetics in art contribute to the rich tapestry of our cultural landscape, sparking conversations, provoking thought, and enriching our lives with visual and sensory pleasure. By embracing and celebrating aesthetics, we foster a deeper appreciation for the diverse and transformative power of art in our culture.

~

Alla Prima

Alla prima is a painting technique that involves completing a work in one sitting, without allowing the paint to dry in between layers. It is a direct and spontaneous approach to painting, where the artist applies wet paint onto wet paint, resulting in a fresh and immediate appearance. This technique allows for a sense of energy and vitality in the artwork, as the artist is able to capture the essence of the subject in a single session.

Alla prima is important to arts and culture as it offers a unique and expressive way of creating art. It allows artists to work quickly and intuitively, capturing the moment and the emotions associated with it. This technique is often associated with plein air painting, where artists paint outdoors to capture the changing light and atmosphere.

Alla prima paintings have a sense of immediacy and spontaneity that can be captivating to viewers, as they can witness the artist's process and the energy that went into creating the artwork. It also challenges traditional methods of layering and building up a painting, offering a fresh and contemporary approach to art-making.

~

Allegory

Allegory is like a hidden message in a story or artwork that uses symbols and imagery to represent deeper meanings. It's kind of like a puzzle that you have to solve to understand what the artist or writer is trying to say. For example, in a book or movie, a character might represent an idea or a concept, like love or freedom. By using allegory, artists and writers can explore complex ideas and emotions in a way that's more interesting and thought-provoking. It's important to arts and culture because it allows us to express and understand things that might be difficult to put into words or show directly. It adds depth and layers to our experiences with art, and it encourages us to think critically and interpret things in our own unique ways.

Allegory is super important to arts and culture because it helps us connect with and understand the world around us in a different way. It's like a secret language that artists and writers use to communicate their ideas and feelings. It can make us think about things in new and unexpected ways, and it can challenge our assumptions and beliefs. In a world where we're constantly bombarded with information and messages, allegory gives us a chance to slow down and really engage with art on a deeper level. It encourages us to ask questions, to explore different perspectives, and to find our own meaning in the things we see and experience. So, whether you're into movies, books, paintings, or any other form of art, allegory is a powerful tool that can enrich your understanding and appreciation of the world around you.

~

Appropriation

Appropriation is when an artist takes elements from another artist's work and incorporates them into their own. It can involve borrowing images, styles, or techniques and recontextualizing them in a new way. This can be seen as a form of homage, critique, or commentary on the original work.

In arts and culture, appropriation is important because it allows artists to engage with and respond to existing works, traditions, and ideas. It can spark conversations about originality, authorship, and cultural exchange. It also challenges notions of ownership and the boundaries of creativity. By appropriating and reinterpreting existing works, artists can create new meanings and perspectives, pushing the boundaries of what is considered art. This can lead to innovative and thought-provoking creations that contribute to the ongoing evolution of arts and culture.

~

Artifice

Artifice, in the context of art, refers to the deliberate use of skill, technique, and creativity to create illusions, simulations, or intentional contrivances within an artwork. It's like the intentional manipulation or deviation from reality to convey a specific message, challenge perceptions, or provoke thought.

Artifice allows artists to question, subvert, and reimagine the boundaries of artistic representation. By intentionally employing artifice, artists challenge the notion of objective reality and invite viewers to question their own assumptions and biases. Artifice can be used to create thought-provoking narratives, explore conceptual ideas, or critique societal constructs. It encourages us to critically engage with the artwork, unraveling layers of meaning and embracing the imaginative possibilities of artistic expression.

Artifice sparks discussions, pushes boundaries, and fosters a deeper understanding of the complexities of our culture and human experience. By appreciating and understanding artifice, we acknowledge the power of art to transcend reality, challenge conventions, and reshape our perception of the world. Artifice is a testament to the transformative nature of art, encouraging us to question and **reima**gine the **possibi**lities **with**in our **cult**ure and **ourse**lves.

~

Avant Garde

Avant-garde is a term used **to desc**ribe **innov**ative and **experi**mental art **that pus**hes the **bound**aries of **tradit**ional **nor**ms and **conven**tions. **It is often assoc**iated with **arti**sts **who** are **ahe**ad of **their** time and **chall**enge the **stat**us quo. **Avant-garde** art can **ta**ke many **for**ms, **inclu**ding **vis**ual art, **mus**ic, **liter**ature, and **perfor**mance art. **It is impor**tant to **arts** and **cult**ure **beca**use it **encou**rages **creat**ivity, **explor**ation, **and** the **develo**pment of new **ide**as.

Avant-garde artists **often bre**ak **free** from **establ**ished **rul**es and **expect**ations, **allow**ing **for** the **emerg**ence of **fre**sh **perspec**tives and the **evolu**tion of **arti**stic **move**ments. **Their** work can **insp**ire and **influ**ence **futu**re **genera**tions of **arti**sts, **shap**ing the **cour**se of art **hist**ory and **contri**buting to the **div**ersity and **rich**ness of **arti**stic **expre**ssion.

~

Background

Background **ref**ers to the **part of** an **artw**ork that **appe**ars **farth**est **from** the **view**er. **It's** like the **suppo**rting **cast** that **sets** the **stag**e for the **main subj**ects or **obje**cts in a **compos**ition. **Imag**ine it as the **back**drop or **sett**ing of a **pain**ting, **photo**graph, **or** any **vis**ual **artw**ork. **The backg**round **prov**ides **cont**ext, **atmos**phere, and **a sense**

of space, enhancing the overall story and creating a complete visual experience.

Background plays a crucial role in arts and culture as it helps establish the mood, environment, and narrative of an artwork. It sets the scene, whether it's a serene landscape, a bustling cityscape, or an abstract space, and contributes to the overall aesthetic appeal. The background can create a sense of depth, making the foreground subjects stand out and appear more prominent. It also allows artists to convey symbolism and convey messages subtly, adding layers of meaning to the artwork.

By paying attention to the background, artists can transport viewers into different worlds, evoke emotions, and spark their imagination. Understanding and appreciating the background in art enriches our cultural experiences and enhances our ability to interpret and connect with the stories being told on the canvas or within any visual medium.

~

Balance

Balance, in the realm of art, refers to the harmonious distribution of visual elements within an artwork. It's like finding the perfect equilibrium that creates a sense of stability and aesthetic satisfaction. Think of balance as the artistic tightrope act where different elements like color, shape, size, and composition are carefully arranged to create a visually pleasing and cohesive whole.

Balance is of utmost importance in arts and culture because it provides a sense of order, unity, and visual appeal to an artwork. It allows artists to create a composition where no single element overwhelms or dominates the others, ensuring that every part contributes meaningfully to the whole. Through balance, artists can guide the viewer's eye and create a sense of stability, making the artwork visually engaging and harmonious.

Balance can be achieved in various ways, such as symmetrical balance where elements are evenly distributed, or asymmetrical balance where visual weight is distributed differently but still creates equilibrium. By understanding and utilizing balance, artists can create captivating visuals that evoke emotions, communicate messages, and enhance the overall artistic experience. Moreover, balance encourages viewers to engage with the artwork, as it creates a sense of visual satisfaction and invites exploration. Appreciating and recognizing balance in art fosters a deeper understanding and enjoyment of artistic expression in our cultural landscape.

~

Blue Chip

Blue chip art refers to artworks by highly esteemed and established artists that have gained significant recognition, value, and market demand. It's like the top-tier, highly sought-after artworks that are considered prestigious within the art world.

Blue chip art holds immense importance in arts and culture as it represents the pinnacle of artistic achievement and influence within the art market.

Blue chip artworks are created by renowned artists who have made a lasting impact on the art world through their innovation, originality, and artistic excellence. These artworks often become iconic, setting trends, and influencing future generations of artists. Blue chip art represents a significant cultural and historical value, serving as a reflection of our society's artistic evolution and values.

Additionally, blue chip art plays a vital role in the art market, driving the economy and acting as an investment for collectors and institutions. By understanding and appreciating blue chip art, we gain insight into the legacy and impact of influential artists, contribute to ongoing conversations about artistic value and market dynamics, and celebrate the enduring power of art to inspire, captivate, and shape our culture.

~

Brushwork

Brushwork refers to the way an artist applies paint to a canvas using a brush. It is an essential element of painting that can greatly influence the overall look and feel of a piece. Brushwork can vary in terms of the size, shape, and texture of the brush used, as well as the pressure and speed at which the paint is applied. It can be loose and expressive, creating bold and energetic strokes, or it can be precise and controlled, resulting in delicate and detailed lines.

Brushwork is important to arts and culture because it allows artists to convey their emotions, thoughts, and ideas through the physical act of painting. It adds depth, texture, and movement to a piece, enhancing its visual impact and creating a unique artistic style.

Brushwork also plays a role in the historical context of art, as different brushwork techniques have been associated with different artistic movements and periods. By studying and appreciating brushwork, we can gain a deeper understanding of the artistic process and the evolution of art throughout history.

~

Canon

Canon refers to a set of established works, artists, or practices that are widely recognized, respected, and considered as important or influential within a specific artistic tradition, period, or genre. It's like a curated collection of artworks or artists that are considered significant and enduring in their impact on artistic expression.

Canon holds significant importance in arts and culture as it serves as a reference point, a source of inspiration, and a framework for understanding and appreciating artistic achievements. The canon provides a shared cultural heritage and a foundation for artistic discourse and analysis. It helps us trace the development and evolution of artistic movements, styles, and ideas over time.

The canon elevates certain artworks and artists to the status of cultural icons, influencing future generations of creators and shaping artistic norms and standards. It guides our understanding of quality, excellence, and artistic value.

However, it is also important to critically examine and challenge the canon, ensuring representation and inclusion of diverse voices and perspectives. By understanding and engaging with the canon, we gain insight into the rich tapestry of artistic expression, discover connections between different works and artists, and contribute to the ongoing dialogue and evolution of arts and culture.

~

Chiaroscuro

Chiaroscuro is a technique used in visual arts, particularly in painting, to create a strong contrast between light and dark. It involves the skillful use of light and shadow to give depth and volume to a composition. The term "chiaroscuro" comes from the Italian words "chiaro" meaning light and "scuro" meaning dark. This technique has been used by artists throughout history to create dramatic and realistic effects in their artwork.

Chiaroscuro adds depth and dimension to a composition, making it more visually interesting and engaging. It can evoke different emotions and moods, depending on how it is used. For example, strong contrasts of light and dark can create a sense of drama and tension, while softer transitions can create a more peaceful and serene atmosphere. Chiaroscuro also helps to create a sense of realism in artwork, as it mimics the way light falls on objects in the real world. By understanding and using chiaroscuro, artists can enhance their ability to communicate their ideas and emotions through their artwork.

~

Color Theory

Color theory is the study of how colors interact with each other and how they can be used to create different visual effects. It explores concepts such as color harmony, contrast, and the psychological impact of different colors.

Understanding color theory is important in arts and culture because it allows artists to effectively communicate their ideas and emotions through the use of color. By understanding how colors work together, artists can create visually pleasing compositions and evoke specific moods or feelings in their audience. Additionally, color theory is also important in fields such as graphic design and advertising, where the strategic use of color can greatly impact the effectiveness of a message or brand.

In arts and culture, color theory is not only important for artists, but also for viewers and consumers of art. By understanding the principles of color theory, viewers can better appreciate and interpret artworks. They can recognize the intentional use of color and understand how it contributes to the overall meaning and impact of the artwork. Color theory also plays a role in our everyday lives, as it influences our preferences and perceptions of color in various contexts, such as fashion, interior design, and even the colors used in movies and advertisements. It's a fundamental aspect of arts and culture that enhances our understanding and enjoyment of visual aesthetics.

~

Composition

Composition in the context of the arts refers to the arrangement and organization of visual elements within a work of art. It involves the careful placement of shapes, lines, colors, and other elements to create a harmonious and balanced whole. Composition is important in arts and culture because it helps to convey the artist's intended message or evoke a specific emotional response from the viewer. A well-composed artwork can guide the viewer's eye, create a sense of unity, and enhance the overall impact and effectiveness of the piece.

In addition, composition plays a crucial role in storytelling and visual communication. It helps to establish a focal point, direct the viewer's attention, and create a sense of depth and perspective. By understanding and applying the principles of composition, artists can effectively convey their ideas and narratives, whether it's through a painting, photograph, or any other visual medium. Moreover, composition is a fundamental aspect of art education, as it provides a framework for artists to explore and experiment with different techniques and styles. It allows artists to express their creativity and individuality while also **provi**ding **a com**mon **lang**uage and **underst**anding for **view**ers to **eng**age **with** and **appre**ciate art.

~

Conceptual Art

Conceptual art is an **arti**stic **move**ment **that prior**itizes the **idea or con**cept **beh**ind an **art**work **ov**er its **phys**ical **form or aesth**etic **quali**ties. **It's** like art **that chall**enges **tradit**ional **noti**ons of **arti**stic **prac**tice and **pla**ces **emph**asis on the **under**lying **con**cept, **mess**age, **or intell**ectual **explor**ation.

Conceptual art **hol**ds **imme**nse **impor**tance **beca**use it **pus**hes **the bound**aries of **arti**stic **expre**ssion and **chall**enges **conven**tional **noti**ons of art. **It encou**rages us to **eng**age **with** art **bey**ond its **vis**ual **app**eal, **invit**ing us to **contem**plate the **idea**s and **con**cepts it **pres**ents.

Conceptual **arti**sts **oft**en **emp**loy **var**ious **medi**ums and **appro**aches, **su**ch as **text**, **perfor**mance, **install**ations, and **multi**media, **to** **explore philoso**phical, **soc**ial, or **polit**ical **the**mes. **Conce**ptual art **spa**rks **convers**ations, **encou**rages **crit**ical **thin**king, and **chall**enges our **assum**ptions **abo**ut art and its **purp**ose. **It promp**ts us to **ques**tion **the** role of **the art**ist, **the** **nat**ure of art, **and** our own **relati**onship to it.

By embracing **concep**tual art, we **fost**er a **dee**per **appreci**ation for **the pow**er of **ide**as and **con**cepts in **shap**ing our **underst**anding of art and the **wor**ld. **It expa**nds our **crea**tive **horiz**ons, **encou**rages us **to think out**side the box, and **fue**ls **inno**vation **wit**hin the arts and **cult**ure **lands**cape. **Conce**ptual art **chall**enges us to **see**

art as a catalyst for intellectual and social discourse, offering new perspectives and possibilities for artistic expression.

~

Convergence

Convergence in the context of arts and culture refers to the coming together of different artistic disciplines, styles, or ideas to create something new and unique. It is a process of blending and merging various elements to create a cohesive and harmonious whole. Convergence allows artists to explore new possibilities, challenge traditional norms, and break down barriers between different art forms.

In today's rapidly changing world, convergence is becoming increasingly important in arts and culture. It allows artists to collaborate and combine their skills and perspectives, resulting in innovative and boundary-pushing creations.

Convergence also encourages cross-pollination of ideas, leading to the emergence of new artistic movements and trends. It helps to break down the silos between different art forms and encourages a more inclusive and diverse artistic landscape. By embracing convergence, artists can explore new ways of expression, challenge established norms, and create art that resonates with the ever-evolving tastes and sensibilities of art enthusiasts.

~

Contour

Contour in the context of arts and culture refers to the outline or shape of an object or figure. It is the line that defines the edges and boundaries of a form. Contour drawing is a technique where an artist focuses on capturing the outer edges of an object or figure, without shading or adding details. This technique helps to emphasize the form and structure of the subject.

Contour is important to arts and culture because it allows artists to accurately represent the shape and proportions of objects and figures. By studying and practicing contour drawing, artists can develop their observational skills and improve their ability to capture the essence of a subject.

Contour drawing also helps artists to understand the underlying structure and anatomy of the human body, which is crucial in figurative art. Additionally, contour can be used creatively to convey movement, energy, and emotion in a composition. It adds a sense of depth and dimension to a two-dimensional artwork, making it more engaging and visually appealing.

~

Contrapposto

Contrapposto is a term used in the field of visual arts, particularly in sculpture and painting, to describe a specific pose or stance of a human figure. It refers to the positioning of the body in a way that creates a sense of naturalness and balance. In contrapposto, the weight of the body is shifted onto one leg, causing the hips and shoulders to tilt in opposite directions. This creates a dynamic and lifelike appearance, as if the figure is in the midst of movement or action.

Contrapposto is important to arts and culture because it adds a sense of realism and naturalness to the representation of the human form. By using this technique, artists are able to convey a sense of movement, balance, and grace in their artwork. It allows the viewer to connect with the figure on a deeper level, as it mimics the natural way in which the body moves and stands. Contrapposto has been used throughout history in various art forms, from ancient Greek sculptures to Renaissance paintings, and continues to be a fundamental technique in the study and practice of figurative art.

~

Crypto Art

Crypto art refers to digital artworks that are created, bought, sold, and owned using blockchain technology and cryptocurrencies. It's a new frontier where technology and art intersect, allowing artists to create, share, and monetize their digital creations in unique and innovative ways.

Crypto art holds immense importance in arts and culture as it revolutionizes the way we perceive, distribute, and value art. By leveraging blockchain technology, crypto art provides artists with opportunities for direct ownership, provenance, and authenticity verification of their digital creations. It challenges the traditional notions of art ownership, copyright, and the role of intermediaries in the art market.

Crypto art fosters a global community of artists, collectors, and enthusiasts who engage in the creation, sale, and appreciation of digital artworks. It opens doors for artists to explore new mediums, interactive experiences, and digital aesthetics.

Crypto art also raises questions about the impact of technology on artistic expression, the role of art in the digital age, and the democratization of the art world. By understanding and participating in crypto art, we contribute to the evolution of art as a cultural and economic force, exploring new possibilities for artistic creation, ownership, and engagement. Crypto art challenges us to reimagine the boundaries of art, technology, and culture, shaping the future of artistic expression.

~

Distortion

Distortion refers to the intentional alteration or manipulation of visual elements to create a sense of exaggeration, abstraction, or disorientation. It is often used as a creative technique to evoke emotions, challenge traditional perceptions, or convey a specific message. Distortion can be achieved through various artistic mediums such as painting, photography, sculpture, and digital art.

In arts and culture, distortion plays a significant role in pushing boundaries and breaking away from conventional norms. It allows artists to explore new possibilities, challenge societal norms, and express their unique perspectives.

Distortion can be used to convey a sense of chaos, surrealism, or even to highlight the flaws and imperfections of the human experience. By distorting reality, artists can create thought-provoking and visually captivating works that engage viewers on a deeper level, sparking conversations and encouraging critical thinking. It adds a layer of complexity and intrigue to the artistic landscape, making it an essential element in pushing the boundaries of creativity and expression.

~

Elevation

Elevation, in the realm of art, refers to the depiction of objects or subjects from a high or elevated viewpoint. It's like looking at something from an elevated position, as if we were hovering above it. This perspective provides a unique and often immersive vantage point that offers a bold and intriguing way of experiencing the artwork.

Elevation plays a significant role in arts and culture by offering a fresh perspective and enhancing the visual impact of an artwork. By portraying objects or subjects from an elevated viewpoint, artists can create a sense of grandeur, expansiveness, and depth within their compositions.

Elevation allows us to see things from a unique angle, encouraging us to explore and appreciate the details, relationships, and narratives present in the artwork. It can evoke a sense of awe, curiosity, and wonder as we contemplate the scene from a new perspective. By embracing elevation, artists open up new possibilities for storytelling, interpretation, and engagement, enriching our artistic experiences and expanding our understanding of the world around us. Elevation invites us to look beyond the ordinary and discover the extraordinary in arts and culture.

~

Figurative Art

Figurative art refers to artwork that represents the real world and its objects, people, or scenes in a recognizable and representational manner. It is a style of art that focuses on depicting the human form, objects, or landscapes in a way that is easily identifiable and relatable to the viewer. Figurative art often emphasizes the use of color, form, and composition to create a realistic representation of the subject matter.

Figurative art is important because it allows artists to communicate and express their ideas, emotions, and experiences in a way that is accessible and relatable to a wide audience. It provides a visual language that can be understood and appreciated by people from different backgrounds and cultures. Figurative art also plays a significant role in preserving and documenting the history, traditions, and stories of a particular time and place. It allows us to connect with the past, understand different perspectives, and explore the human condition through visual representation.

~

Focal Point

Focal point, in the context of art, refers to the specific area or element within an artwork that commands the most attention. It's like the eye-catching centerpiece that captures our gaze and becomes the visual focal point of the composition. Think of it as the spotlight shining on a particular subject, object, or detail, drawing us in and guiding our exploration of the artwork.

Focal point is incredibly important in arts and culture because it directs our focus and enhances the overall impact of an artwork. It serves as a visual anchor, providing a clear point of interest that guides the viewer's attention and conveys the artist's intended message. By strategically placing a focal point, artists can create a sense of hierarchy, emphasizing the significance of certain elements or guiding the narrative of the artwork.

The focal point captures our imagination and evokes emotions, allowing us to connect more deeply with the artist's vision and intentions. By understanding and appreciating the focal point, we can interpret the artist's story, explore the layers of meaning, and engage in meaningful dialogue about art and its cultural significance. The focal point encourages us to actively participate in the artistic experience, fostering a deeper appreciation for the richness and diversity of a work of art.

~

Foreground

Foreground refers to the part of an artwork that appears closest to the viewer. It's like the star of the show, the main focus that grabs our attention and takes center stage. Imagine it as the spotlight shining on the most significant subjects or objects in a composition. The foreground holds our gaze and draws us into the artwork, inviting us to explore its details and narratives.

Foreground holds great importance, as it showcases the key elements that the artist wants to emphasize or communicate. It serves as the visual anchor, capturing our attention and setting the tone for the entire artwork. The foreground allows artists to express their intentions, convey emotions, and tell stories by depicting subjects with greater detail, color, and prominence. It creates a sense of immediacy and intimacy, making the viewer feel intimately connected with the artwork.

By understanding and appreciating the foreground, we can better understand the artist's message and the stories being portrayed. The foreground captures our imagination, engages us with its beauty or message, and sparks conversations that deepen our appreciation for art and its ability to reflect and shape our culture.

~

Genre

Genre refers to a category or classification of artistic works that share similar characteristics or themes. It is a way to organize and categorize different forms of art, such as literature, music, film, and visual arts. Genres provide a framework for artists and audiences to understand and appreciate different styles and expressions within a particular medium. They allow artists to explore and experiment within established conventions, while also providing audiences with a sense of familiarity and expectation.

In literature, the genre we pick determines whether we're going to outer space or investigating that strange sound coming from the basement. In dance, the genre lets us know whether to pirouette or to break dance. In cinema, the genre might tug at our heartstrings or ready us for battle. And in art, the same scene painted in different genres might reflect our reality or our alternate reality.

Genre differentiation is important because it helps to create a sense of identity and community within artistic communities. It provides a common language and framework for artists to communicate and collaborate with one another. Genres also play a role in shaping cultural and societal norms, as they reflect and respond to the values, beliefs, and experiences of a particular time and place. Additionally, genres allow audiences to navigate and discover new works of art that align with their personal preferences and interests. They provide a sense of comfort and familiarity, while also offering opportunities for exploration and discovery.

~

Glazing

Glazing refers to a technique used in painting where a transparent layer of paint is applied over a dried layer of paint. This technique allows for the creation of various effects such as depth, luminosity, and texture. Glazing can be done with different types of paint, including oil, acrylic, and watercolor.

Glazing adds richness and complexity to a painting. By layering transparent colors over each other, artists can create subtle shifts in tone and color that give depth and dimension to their work. This technique has been used by artists throughout history, from the Renaissance masters to contemporary painters, and it continues to be a valuable tool for artists to express their creativity and vision. Glazing also allows artists to achieve a level of realism and luminosity that is difficult to achieve with other painting techniques, making it an important skill for artists to master.

~

Impressionism

Impressionism is an artistic movement that emerged in the late 19th century. It is characterized by its emphasis on capturing the fleeting and subjective impressions of a scene or subject, rather than aiming for precise and realistic representation. Impressionist artists often used loose brushstrokes, vibrant colors, and unconventional compositions to convey their personal interpretations of light, atmosphere, and movement.

Impressionism revolutionized the way art was created and perceived. Prior to Impressionism, the dominant artistic style was realism, which aimed for accurate and detailed representation. However, Impressionism challenged these conventions and introduced a new way of seeing and experiencing the world.

By focusing on the artist's subjective impressions and emotions, Impressionism brought a sense of individuality and personal expression to art. It also paved the way for further artistic experimentation and the development of other modern art movements. Today, Impressionism continues to inspire and influence artists, and its impact on the art world is undeniable.

~

Medium

In the arts, a medium is the material or form that an artist uses to create their work. For example, a painter might use oil paint on canvas, a sculptor might use clay, and a filmmaker might use film. The medium can have a big impact on the way a work of art is perceived by the viewer. A painting made with oil paint is likely to look different than a painting made with watercolors. The medium an artist uses is influential because it can help to convey the artist's message. Sculptors might use clay to create a work that is meant to be fragile and temporary, while filmmakers might use film or storytelling to create a work that is meant to be immersive and realistic.

The medium can influence the way the work is perceived by the viewer, and it can help to convey the artist's message. The use of new and experimental mediums allows artists to explore different ways of expressing themselves and to keep the arts relevant in a rapidly changing world. The rise of digital art has allowed artists to create works that are interactive and immersive. This has opened up new possibilities for artists to tell stories and to engage with viewers in new ways. In a world that is increasingly dominated by technology, artists are pursuing new mediums to connect with audiences and can help to keep the arts fresh in the 21st century.

~

Middle Ground

Middle ground is an art term that refers to the visual space between the foreground and the background in a composition. It's like the sweet spot that balances the elements in a piece of artwork. Think of it as the cozy spot where things are not too close or too far away, but just right in the middle.

In terms of a painting, for example, the middle ground is where objects or subjects are depicted with moderate detail and size, neither dominating the forefront nor receding into the background. It creates a sense of depth and perspective, making the artwork visually engaging and inviting the viewer to explore the space within.

The concept of middle ground is vital to arts and culture because it allows artists to create a harmonious and balanced composition. It enables them to guide the viewer's eye and create a sense of depth and realism in their work. Without middle ground, art could feel flat and lacking dimension. It gives artists the opportunity to establish a visual hierarchy, drawing attention to important elements while maintaining a cohesive overall image.

The middle ground also encourages viewers to actively engage with the artwork, as their eyes are naturally drawn to explore the space between the foreground and background. By **understanding** and **utilizing** the **middle** ground, **artists** can **create captivating visuals** that **evoke emotions, convey narratives,** and **spark meaningful connections between** the **audience** and the **artwork.**

~

Narrative

Narrative is the **telling** of a **story** or the **depiction** of a **sequence** of **events** through **various artistic mediums** such as **literature, film, theater,** and **visual arts.** It is an **essential element** in **arts** and **culture** as it **allows artists** to **communicate their ideas, emotions,** and **experiences** in **a structured** and **engaging manner.**

Narrative art plays a **crucial role** in **arts** and **culture** as it **enables individuals** to **connect with** and **understand different perspectives, cultures,** and **historical events.** **Through narratives, artists** can **explore complex themes, challenge societal norms,** and **provoke thought** and **discussion.** It **allows** for the **exploration of personal** and **collective identities,** as **well** as the **expression of diverse voices** and **experiences.**

Additionally, narratives have the **power** to **evoke emotions, create empathy,** and **foster a sense of community** and **shared understanding among individuals. By engaging with narratives, people** can **develop critical thinking skills, expand their knowledge** and **cultural awareness,** and **gain a deeper appreciation** for the **arts.**

~

Negative Space

Negative space refers to the empty or unoccupied areas surrounding the main subject or objects in a work of art. It is the space that is not filled with the primary elements of the composition, such as figures, objects, or patterns. Negative space plays a crucial role in creating balance, harmony, and visual interest in a piece of art.

Negative space is important because it allows for the creation of a dynamic and visually engaging composition. By intentionally leaving areas of the artwork empty, artists can draw attention to the main subject or objects, emphasizing their importance and creating a sense of focus. Negative space also helps to define the shape and form of the main subject, as the surrounding empty areas can act as a contrasting backdrop.

Additionally, negative space can evoke emotions and convey meaning in a subtle and abstract manner, allowing viewers to interpret and engage with the artwork on a deeper level. Overall, negative space is a powerful tool that artists use to enhance the visual impact and storytelling potential of their creations.

~

Perspective

Perspective is a fundamental concept in the arts that refers to the way we perceive and interpret the world around us. It involves our unique point of view, influenced by our experiences, beliefs, and emotions. In simpler terms, perspective is like wearing a pair of glasses that shapes how we see and understand things.

In the context of arts and culture, perspective is crucial because it allows artists to express their individuality and convey their messages in a meaningful way. It adds depth and complexity to their work, making it more relatable and thought-provoking for everyone.

By exploring different perspectives, artists can challenge societal norms, spark conversations, and inspire empathy among viewers. Perspective also encourages critical thinking and open-mindedness, enabling us to appreciate diverse cultures, ideas, and artistic expressions. Using perspective in various ways empowers artists to question the status quo and contribute to the ever-evolving landscape of arts and culture.

~

Photorealism

Photorealism is a style of art that aims to create paintings, drawings, or sculptures that closely resemble high-resolution photographs. It emerged in the late 1960s and early 1970s as a reaction against abstract expressionism and other non-representational art movements.

Photorealism requires great technical skill and attention to detail, as artists strive to capture every nuance and texture with precision. This style of art is important because it challenges our perception of reality and blurs the line between the real and the reproduced. It allows artists to explore the boundaries of representation and pushes the limits of what can be achieved through artistic skill and technique. By creating hyper-realistic images, photorealism invites viewers to question their own perception and engage with the art on a deeper level.

In addition to its technical prowess, photorealism also holds cultural significance. It reflects the advancements in technology and the increasing prevalence of photography in our daily lives. With the rise of digital photography and social media platforms, we are constantly bombarded with images that claim to depict reality. Photorealism challenges this notion by demonstrating that even the most realistic images can be meticulously crafted by human hands. It reminds us that art is not just about capturing a moment, but also about the artist's interpretation and skill. By appreciating photorealistic art, we can gain a deeper understanding of the power of observation, interpretation, and the impact of technology on our perception of reality.

~

Plein Air

Plein air is a term used in the arts to describe the act of painting or drawing outdoors, directly from the natural environment. It originated in the 19th century with the Impressionist movement and has since become a popular practice among artists of various styles. Plein air allows artists to capture the true essence of a scene, as they are able to observe and interpret the ever-changing light, colors, and atmosphere in real time.

Plein air painting not only provides artists with a unique and immersive experience, but it also plays a significant role in arts and culture. By creating art in the open air, artists are able to connect with nature and the surrounding environment in a more intimate way. This practice encourages artists to observe and appreciate the beauty of the world around them, fostering a deeper understanding and connection to the natural world.

Additionally, plein air paintings often capture the unique characteristics and cultural aspects of a specific location, serving as a visual documentation of a particular time and place. These artworks can evoke a sense of nostalgia and preserve the history and heritage of a region, making plein air an important part of arts and culture.

~

Proportion

Proportion is a concept in the arts that refers to the size, scale, and relationship of different elements within a work of art. It helps create a sense of balance, harmony, and realism in a piece. Proportion allows artists to accurately depict the relationships between objects, figures, and spaces, making their work more visually appealing and relatable to the viewer.

In art, proportion is crucial for creating a sense of realism and believability. When objects or figures are proportionate, they appear more natural and lifelike, enhancing the overall quality of the artwork. Proportion also plays a role in creating visual interest and balance within a composition. By carefully considering the proportions of different elements, artists can create a harmonious and visually pleasing arrangement that captures the viewer's attention.

Understanding proportion allows artists to manipulate and distort it for creative purposes, leading to unique and innovative artistic expressions. Overall, proportion is a fundamental concept in the arts that helps artists communicate their ideas effectively and engage viewers on a deeper level.

~

Realism

Realism is an artistic style that aims to depict subjects in a truthful and accurate manner, often emphasizing the details and capturing the essence of the subject. It emerged in the mid-19th century as a reaction against the idealized and romanticized depictions of the previous art movements. Realism seeks to portray the world as it is, without embellishments or distortions, and often focuses on everyday life, ordinary people, and social issues.

Realism is important to arts and culture because it provides a window into the realities of different time periods and societies. It allows us to understand and appreciate the nuances of the human experience, as well as the social, political, and cultural contexts in which art is created.

Realist artworks can evoke empathy, provoke thought, and challenge our preconceived notions. By presenting the world in a truthful and unfiltered way, realism encourages us to question and engage with the world around us, fostering a deeper understanding and connection to our own lives and the lives of others.

~

Red Chip

Red chip art refers to emerging or mid-career artists whose work shows significant potential and is gaining recognition within the art world. It's like the up-and-coming artists who are making waves and attracting attention for their innovative approaches and artistic talent.

Red chip art holds importance in arts and culture as it represents the future of artistic expression and the evolving landscape of creativity. Red chip artists bring fresh perspectives, experimentation, and new ideas to the forefront, pushing boundaries and challenging established norms. Their work reflects the contemporary issues, concerns, and aesthetics of our time. Red chip art is a reflection of the diverse voices and emerging trends within the art world, highlighting the cultural, social, and political conversations of today.

By recognizing and supporting red chip art, we contribute to the growth and development of the artistic community, fostering a nurturing environment for creativity to thrive. Red chip art encourages us to explore and engage with the artistic expressions of emerging talents, promoting inclusivity, diversity, and the constant evolution of arts and culture. It provides an opportunity to discover exciting new artists and contribute to the ongoing dialogue surrounding contemporary artistic practices.

~

Review

In the arts and culture world, a review is a report card for movies, books, music, art shows. It shares a critic's thoughts and feelings about that creative masterpiece. Reviews help you decide what to check out or avoid, just like a compass guiding you to the coolest artworks and cultural events, or steering you away from not-so-great ones.

Reviews can help us celebrate the greatness of talented creators. This is because reviews can highlight the strengths of a work of art, and give credit to the people who created it. They provide feedback to the artists who might learn and grow. It's not smack-talk. The whole thing brings art communities together for assessments.

Reviews are vital in the arts and culture world because they let us celebrate the greatness of talented creators and also improve what they make. When artists get feedback through reviews, they can learn what shines bright in their work and what might need a little polish. Plus, as arts fans, reviews connect us to a whole community of like-minded peeps who share our passions. They allow us to discuss things in both a positive and negative way, enriching our opinion of a work of art and our experience with it.

~

Scale

Scale is a concept in the arts that refers to the size and proportion of objects in relation to each other and their surroundings. It is a crucial element in creating visual impact and conveying meaning in art. In art, scale can be used to emphasize certain elements or ideas, create a sense of depth or distance, or evoke specific emotions.

For example, a large-scale sculpture can command attention and create a sense of awe, while a small-scale painting can invite viewers to lean in and examine the details. Scale also plays a role in creating a sense of realism or abstraction in art, as artists can manipulate the size of objects to distort or enhance their representation.

In addition to its visual impact, scale is influential because it helps us understand and interpret the world around us. By observing and analyzing the scale of objects in art, we can gain insights into the relationships between different elements, the significance of certain subjects, and the overall composition of a piece.

Scale can also be used to challenge our perceptions and expectations, inviting us to question our assumptions and explore new perspectives. Overall, scale is a powerful tool that artists use to communicate ideas, evoke emotions, and engage viewers in a meaningful and thought-provoking way.

~

Subject

The **subject** is the main focus or theme of a work of art. It is the central idea or topic that the artist is trying to convey or explore through their creative expression. The subject can be a person, an object, a landscape, an emotion, or even an abstract concept.

Having a prominent subject allows artists to communicate their thoughts, feelings, and perspectives to the audience. By choosing a specific subject, artists can create a narrative, evoke emotions, or make a statement about the world around them. The subject of a work of art can also reflect the cultural, social, and historical context in which it was created, providing insights into different time periods and societies.

Understanding the subject of a work of art helps viewers engage with and interpret the artwork. It allows them to connect with the artist's intentions and gain a deeper appreciation for the piece. The subject can spark conversations, challenge societal norms, and inspire new ideas. In addition, the subject of a work of art can also serve as a form of documentation, capturing moments in history or representing different aspects of human experience. The subject plays a crucial role in arts and culture by serving as a vehicle for expression, communication, and reflection.

~

Sfumato

Sfumato is a painting technique that involves the gradual blending of colors and tones to create a soft, hazy effect. It was famously used by Leonardo da Vinci in his masterpiece, the Mona Lisa. This technique adds depth and dimension to a painting, creating a sense of atmosphere and mystery. In the arts, sfumato is used to create realistic and lifelike representations of the world. By subtly blending colors and tones, artists can capture the subtle nuances of light and shadow, creating a sense of depth and realism in their work. This technique has been used by artists throughout history and continues to be a valuable tool in the world of art.

In addition to its technical importance, sfumato also has cultural significance. It is often associated with the Renaissance period, a time of great artistic and intellectual achievement. The use of sfumato in paintings from this era reflects the desire to capture the beauty and complexity of the natural world. It also represents a shift towards a more realistic and humanistic approach to art, as artists sought to depict the world as they saw it, rather than relying on idealized or symbolic representations. Sfumato, therefore, not only enhances the visual appeal of a work of art but also carries with it a rich historical and cultural context that adds depth and meaning to the artwork.

~

Texture

Texture is the visual or tactile quality of a surface within an artwork. It's like the "feel" of the artwork, whether we can physically touch it or not. Texture adds depth, dimension, and a sensory experience to the visual representation, creating a captivating and immersive artistic encounter.

Texture holds immense importance for art because it enhances our sensory engagement and adds richness to the artistic experience. It allows us to visually and emotionally connect with the artwork on a deeper level. Artists use different techniques, materials, and brushstrokes to create various textures, ranging from smooth and polished to rough and rugged.

Use of texture can evoke a wide range of emotions, from the comfort of a soft fabric to the roughness of weathered wood. It adds layers of interest, realism, and visual intrigue to the artwork. Texture also invites us to explore and appreciate the intricate details, patterns, and surfaces within the artwork, fostering a deeper connection with the artist's creative process. By understanding and appreciating texture, we can unlock new dimensions of meaning, sensory experiences, and appreciation for the diverse forms of artistic expression in our culture.

~

Theme

Theme refers to the central idea, message, or concept conveyed by an artwork. It's like the underlying thread that ties everything together and provides a unifying focus for the artistic expression. Themes can be broad or specific, representing a range of subjects, emotions, or concepts explored within the artwork.

Theme holds significant importance in arts and culture as it provides a deeper layer of meaning and resonance to the artwork or event. It serves as a guiding force that shapes the artists' or performers' visions and resonates with the audience. Themes can evoke emotions, provoke thoughts, and challenge our perspectives, allowing us to connect with the artwork on a personal and universal level.

By exploring different themes, artists contribute to the cultural dialogue, addressing social issues, personal experiences, historical events, or philosophical concepts. Themes encourage us to reflect, question, and engage with the world around us. They ignite conversations, bridge cultural gaps, and foster a sense of shared understanding and empathy. By understanding and appreciating the theme of an artwork, we gain insight into the artist's perspective, stimulate our own creativity, and develop a deeper appreciation for the diverse themes that shape the artistic landscape of our culture.

~

Triptych

Triptych is a composition that consists of three separate panels or sections that are displayed together as a single artwork. It's a storytelling format where each panel contributes to a larger narrative or visual exploration. Triptychs have been used throughout history and across various artistic mediums, including painting, photography, and digital art.

Triptychs offer a unique and dynamic way of presenting and experiencing artwork. They provide artists with an expanded canvas to explore complex themes, stories, or visual relationships. Each panel of a triptych can represent different perspectives, moments in time, or symbolic elements that collectively create a cohesive whole. Triptychs invite viewers to actively engage with the artwork, moving their gaze from one panel to another, observing the connections and interactions between the individual parts. They encourage contemplation, interpretation, and a deeper understanding of the artist's intention.

Triptychs also allow for flexibility in display, offering opportunities for spatial arrangement and experimentation. By understanding and appreciating the triptych format, we can appreciate the narrative and compositional possibilities it presents, enriching our artistic encounters and fostering a deeper appreciation for the diverse ways in which art can be expressed and experienced.

~

Trompe L'Oeil

Trompe l'oeil, a French term meaning "deceive the eye," is an artistic technique that creates an optical illusion, making two-dimensional artworks appear three-dimensional or realistic. It's like a visual trick that challenges our perception and blurs the line between reality and art. Trompe l'oeil has been used in various artistic mediums, including painting, murals, and even street art.

Trompe l'oeil holds great power because it captivates and engages viewers through its clever manipulation of perception. By skillfully employing techniques like shading, perspective, and meticulous attention to detail, artists can create incredibly lifelike and immersive artworks.

Trompe l'oeil invites us to question what is real and what is artifice, challenging our understanding of the visual world. It stimulates our curiosity, wonder, and appreciation for the technical mastery involved in creating such convincing illusions. Trompe l'oeil artworks often spark conversations, inviting viewers to marvel at the artistic skill while contemplating the nature of perception and representation. By understanding and appreciating trompe l'oeil, we gain a deeper appreciation for the ingenuity and creativity of artists, expanding our artistic horizons and encouraging us to see the world with new eyes.

~

Underpainting

Underpainting is the initial layer of paint applied to a canvas or surface before adding subsequent layers of color and detail. It's like the foundation that sets the groundwork for the final artwork. Underpainting is often executed in monochromatic or limited color tones and serves as a guide for the artist's composition and values.

Underpainting plays a significant role in arts and culture as it establishes the structure, depth, and tonal values of an artwork. It allows artists to plan and refine their composition, making decisions about light and shadow, form, and overall balance. Underpainting helps artists create a solid foundation for the subsequent layers of color, enhancing the visual impact and realism of the final piece. It also provides a starting point for exploring different artistic styles and techniques.

Underpainting can be transparent or opaque, depending on the desired effect and medium used. By understanding and appreciating underpainting, we gain insight into the artistic process, witnessing the transformation from a blank canvas to a fully realized artwork. It encourages us to appreciate the careful planning and craftsmanship behind an artwork, deepening our connection to the artistic journey and the rich diversity of artistic expression in our culture.

~

Vanishing Point

Vanishing point, in the realm of art, refers to a specific point on the horizon line where parallel lines appear to converge or meet. It's like a visual anchor that guides our perception of depth and perspective in a two-dimensional artwork. The vanishing point is an essential element in creating realistic representations of three-dimensional space.

Vanishing points are interesting because they enable artists to create the illusion of depth and spatial relationships within their artworks. By utilizing vanishing points, artists can accurately depict the way objects recede into the distance, giving a sense of realism and proportion.

The vanishing point allows viewers to immerse themselves in the artwork, as it guides their gaze and creates a visual pathway. Understanding vanishing points enhances our appreciation for the technical skill and precision employed by artists to create convincing and engaging compositions. Vanishing points are utilized in various art forms, including painting, drawing, and digital art, and contribute to our perception and interpretation of the world around us. By recognizing and appreciating the use of vanishing points, we gain a deeper understanding of the visual language and techniques employed by artists, fostering a greater appreciation for the depth and richness of arts in our society.

~

CHAPTER 6 ✿ WTF Is... (Of Course We Mean "What the Fresco?")

~

An Art Gallery

An art gallery is a space dedicated to exhibiting and showcasing visual art, including paintings, sculptures, photographs, installations, and more. It is a venue for artists to present their work to the public and for visitors to engage with and appreciate various forms of artistic expression. Galleries are free to enter, and the gallerists love to talk with visitors about the artists represented and the artworks on display.

Art galleries can offer several interesting aspects for you:

-- Visual Stimulation: Art galleries provide a visually stimulating environment where you can encounter diverse and thought-provoking artworks. They offer an opportunity to engage with different artistic styles, techniques, and themes. Exploring galleries can expose you to a wide range of visual aesthetics, from traditional to contemporary, and can expand your understanding and appreciation of art.

-- Self-Expression and Identity: Art galleries often feature works that explore social issues, personal narratives, and cultural identities. You may resonate with artworks that address topics like diversity, inclusivity, gender, mental health, or environmental concerns. Art can provide a powerful medium for self-expression, storytelling, and reflection, and galleries can serve as spaces where you can explore and relate to these narratives.

-- Interactive Installations: Many contemporary art galleries incorporate interactive and immersive installations that allow visitors to engage with the artwork in a hands-on manner.

-- Technology: Art galleries often embrace digital platforms and social media to reach a wider audience. They may have virtual exhibitions, online collections, or interactive websites that allow you to explore artworks digitally and engage with them beyond the physical gallery space.

Don't hesitate to visit local art galleries, attend art events, and follow artists and galleries on social media to stay updated on exhibitions, emerging artists, and art-related activities. Embrace the opportunity to explore, question, and appreciate the world of art and contribute to the ongoing dialogue and evolution of artistic expression.

~

A Museum

A museum is a space dedicated to the collection, preservation, exhibition, and interpretation of objects or artworks that have historical, cultural, scientific, or artistic significance. Museums can house a wide range of exhibits, including artifacts, paintings, sculptures, photographs, interactive displays, and more. They provide an opportunity to explore and learn about various subjects and aspects of human history and creativity.

There are several reasons why museums can be interesting and engaging for you:

-- Diversity of Exhibits: Museums cover a vast array of topics, ranging from history, science, and technology to art, music, and pop culture. This diversity allows you to find exhibits that align with your interests and passions. Whether you're interested in ancient civilizations, contemporary art, space exploration, or social movements, you can likely find a museum that caters to your preferences.

-- Interactive and Technological Experiences: Many museums today embrace interactive technologies to create immersive and engaging experiences. Virtual reality, augmented reality, touchscreens, and multimedia installations are often integrated into exhibits, making them more dynamic and interactive.

-- Social and Cultural Context: Museums provide insights into different cultures, traditions, and historical events. Exploring diverse exhibitions can help broaden your understanding of the world, fostering empathy and promoting cross-cultural understanding.

-- Learning Opportunities: Museums are educational spaces that offer opportunities for informal learning. They often provide detailed information, engaging narratives, and expert-led tours or audio guides that help you deepen your knowledge on various subjects.

-- Inspiring Creativity: Museums can be a source of

inspiration for your own creative endeavors. Observing art, design, and innovative exhibitions can stimulate your imagination, expand your creative thinking, and expose you to different artistic styles and techniques.

Remember, museums are not just about passive observation. Engage with the exhibits, ask questions, participate in activities, and share your experiences through social media or online platforms. Your unique perspective can contribute to shaping the future of museums by encouraging them to adapt and evolve to cater to the interests and preferences of your generation.

~

A Biennale

The term "Biennale" refers to a major international art exhibition that takes place every two years. It originated from the Venice Biennale (La Biennale di Venezia), which is one of the most prominent and oldest art biennials in the world. The Venice Biennale was first held in 1895 and has since become a prestigious event that showcases contemporary art, architecture, film, dance, and theater.

The Venice Biennale consists of several different components, including the International Art Exhibition, which features curated exhibitions by artists from various countries, and the International Architecture Exhibition, focusing on architectural concepts and projects. In addition to these main exhibitions, the Venice Biennale also hosts specialized events, such as the International Festival of Contemporary Music, the

International Film Festival, and the International Theatre Festival.

The Venice Biennale has inspired the establishment of numerous art biennials and triennials around the world, which are organized by different cities and countries. These events aim to showcase contemporary art, foster cultural exchange, and provide a platform for artists, curators, and art professionals to connect and engage with a global audience.

Examples of other notable biennales include:

-- São Paulo Biennial (São Paulo, Brazil)

-- Documenta (Kassel, Germany)

-- Istanbul Biennial (Istanbul, Turkey)

-- Whitney Biennial (New York City, USA)

-- Sydney Biennale (Sydney, Australia)

~

Spoken Word and Storytelling

Spoken word and storytelling are forms of oral performance where individuals express themselves, share stories, or convey messages through spoken language. While they share some similarities, there are distinct differences between the two:

-- Spoken Word: Spoken word is a performance art form that combines elements of poetry, storytelling, and theater. It involves the recitation or performance of original or pre-existing poetic pieces that are often rhythmic, passionate, and emotionally charged. Spoken word performances may include elements of music, movement, and improvisation, and they often tackle personal experiences, social issues, or political themes. Spoken word can be accompanied by music or performed acapella, and it emphasizes the power of spoken language and vocal delivery to captivate and engage the audience.

-- Storytelling: Storytelling is the art of conveying narratives, tales, or anecdotes orally, typically in a sequential and engaging manner. Storytelling has a long history as a means of passing down cultural traditions, sharing knowledge, and entertaining listeners. Storytellers use their voice, gestures, and expressions to bring characters and events to life, creating vivid mental imagery for the audience. Storytelling can take various forms, including traditional folktales, personal anecdotes, legends, myths, or fictional narratives. It can be performed in intimate settings, such as gatherings or storytelling circles, or on larger stages as a professional performance art.

~

Performance Art

In the enchanting realm where art transcends traditional mediums, performance art reigns supreme. This mesmerizing fusion of visual, auditory, and bodily expressions engulfs audiences in a realm of immersive experiences, igniting emotions and challenging conventions. Originating in the avant-garde movements of the early 20th century, performance art has since blossomed into a tapestry of limitless creativity.

The vibrant history of performance art is punctuated by daring visionaries who dared to defy the norm. From the boundary-pushing provocations of Marina Abramović to the introspective explorations of Yoko Ono, performance art bears witness to fearless artists who use their bodies and voices as powerful instruments of social commentary.

Today, great performance art can be found everywhere, from traditional theaters to bustling city streets and even the digital realm. Immersive installations, interactive spectacles, and thought-provoking durational pieces all contribute to the ever-evolving landscape of this dynamic art form.

A rich tapestry of genres awaits exploration. From visceral body art to politically charged interventions, from intimate one-on-one encounters to grand-scale spectacles, each genre offers a unique lens through which artists can connect, provoke, and captivate their audiences.

Prepare to be transported beyond imagination-performance art continues to challenge boundaries, redefine artistic expression, and illuminate the world with its electrifying presence. So, venture forth and embrace the unexpected of this extraordinary art form.

~

An Exhibition

An exhibition refers to a curated presentation or display of artworks, objects, or collections in a specific space, such as a museum, gallery, cultural institution, or public venue. Exhibitions serve as platforms for artists, curators, and institutions to showcase and share artistic, cultural, historical, or scientific content with the public.

Exhibitions can encompass a wide range of formats and themes, depending on the goals and focus of the organizers. Here are a few common types of exhibitions:

-- Solo Exhibition: A solo exhibition features the works of a single artist, highlighting their artistic practice, themes, or body of work.

-- Group Exhibition: A group exhibition involves the presentation of artworks by multiple artists, often sharing a common theme, concept, or artistic approach.

-- Retrospective Exhibition: A retrospective exhibition showcases an artist's works from their entire artistic career or a significant period, providing an overview of their artistic development and contributions.

-- Thematic or Conceptual Exhibition: Thematic or conceptual exhibitions revolve around a specific theme, concept, or idea rather than focusing on individual artists.

-- Traveling Exhibition: Traveling exhibitions are organized to move from one location to another, often spanning multiple cities or countries.

Exhibitions play a crucial role in promoting artistic and cultural understanding, education, and engagement. They provide opportunities for artists to present their work, curators to explore and interpret artistic concepts, and audiences to experience and appreciate a diverse range of artistic expressions.

~

Cirque du Soleil

Cirque du Soleil Is a unique artistic performance that combines acrobatics, dance, music, and stunning visual effects. It was founded in 1984 in Quebec, Canada by a group of street performers led by Guy Laliberté and Gilles Ste-Croix. They started as a small troupe of performers who put on shows in the streets, but their unique blend of circus arts and street entertainment quickly caught the attention of audiences around the world.

Over the years, Cirque du Soleil has grown into a global phenomenon, with shows that have been seen by millions of people in more than 60 countries. They have won numerous awards for their artistic excellence and have inspired countless performers and artists around the world.

When you arrive at the theater, expect to be greeted by a buzzing atmosphere filled with excitement and anticipation. Make sure to arrive early to get settled in your seat and to take in the pre-show entertainment. You might even get the chance to interact with some of the performers before the show starts!

Cirque du Soleil shows are known for their artistic excellence and attention to detail. The costumes are a feast for the eyes, with intricate designs and vibrant colors that add to the overall visual spectacle. The music is an integral part of the performance, and each show has its unique soundtrack that is composed specifically for that show.

The choreography is often unconventional and experimental, with movements that are inspired by different dance styles from around the world. Makeup is also a crucial part of the show, and each performer has a unique look that is created through makeup.

~

A Vegas Show

For art and art history enthusiasts, Las Vegas offers a unique blend of live performances that showcase exceptional talent and stunning visual effects. Magic shows, burlesque, and impersonators are just a few of the live performances that are available in Las Vegas.

Magic shows like David Copperfield, Penn & Teller, and Criss Angel draw in crowds night after night with their mind-bending illusions and elaborate props. These shows offer a unique form of artistic expression that can be appreciated by art enthusiasts.

Impersonators recreate the iconic performances of famous celebrities like Elvis Presley, Cher, and Frank Sinatra. These shows are accompanied by live music and showcase the performer's incredible talent and attention to detail, making them an excellent choice for art history enthusiasts.

Burlesque shows combine dance, music, and comedy to create a seductive and entertaining experience for the audience. The Performers are often dressed in elaborate costumes, and the shows are known for their sultry and sensual performances.

Overall, Las Vegas offers a diverse range of live performances that can be appreciated by art and art history enthusiasts. These shows showcase exceptional talent and creativity and are a unique form of artistic expression that is sure to leave a lasting impression.

~

A Comedy Club

Hey, happy person! If you're looking for a night of laughs, you gotta check out a comedy club. These venues are the perfect place to unwind and enjoy some hilarious performances.

When you enter a comedy club, expect to be in an intimate setting with a low ceiling, dim lighting, and a stage up front. The audience is usually seated at round tables, and drinks are flowing. You might even catch the smell of popcorn in the air.

During the show, you'll be entertained by a variety of comedians who will make you laugh till your sides hurt. Standup comedy has a rich history that dates back to the early 20th century, and today's comedians continue to push the boundaries with their witty observations on life.

But don't be fooled, it takes a lot of work to be a great comedian. They train for years, writing and testing their material in front of live audiences, trying to perfect their craft. And when they finally hit the stage, they deliver their jokes with impeccable timing and a confidence that only comes from years of practice.

So, whether you're a fan of classic comedians like Richard Pryor and George Carlin or prefer the modern-day humor of Kevin Hart and Ali Wong, a comedy club is the perfect place to experience it all. You'll leave with a smile on your face, feeling like you just spent an evening with your funniest friends.

~

A Music Festival

A music festival is an event where multiple artists and bands perform live music for a large audience. It's a celebration of music and culture, where people come together to enjoy different genres of music, dance, and have fun. Music festivals are important because they provide a platform for emerging artists to showcase their talent, and for established artists to connect with their fans. They also contribute to the local economy by generating revenue for the host city.

The top 10 music festivals in the world are Coachella, Glastonbury, Tomorrowland, Lollapalooza, Roskilde, Primavera Sound, Rock in Rio, Sziget, Electric Daisy Carnival, and Ultra Music Festival. These festivals are held in different parts of the world, such as the United States, Europe, and South America. They usually last for three to five days.

When you go to a music festival, you can expect to see a diverse crowd of people from different backgrounds and cultures. You'll also see various stages with different artists performing simultaneously, food and drink vendors, and merchandise booths. It's important to stay hydrated and wear comfortable clothing and shoes.

Music festivals are critical to arts and culture because they promote creativity, diversity, and inclusivity. They provide a platform for artists to express themselves and connect with their fans. They also bring people together from different parts of the world, creating a sense of community and belonging.

In the music industry, music festivals are significant because they provide a platform for artists to showcase their talent and gain exposure. They also generate attention for the industry, contributing to its growth and development. Overall, music festivals are an important part of our cultural landscape, and they play a vital role in promoting music and arts.

~

An Art Fair

An art fair is a temporary exhibition of art, usually held in a large space like a convention center or warehouse. Art fairs typically feature work by a wide range of artists, including emerging and established artists. They are a great way to see a lot of art in a short amount of time, and to meet and interact with artists.

Art fairs are important for a number of reasons. They help to promote the work of artists, and to connect artists with collectors and other potential buyers. They also help to raise awareness of contemporary art, and to make it more accessible to the public.

Here are the top 10 art fairs in the world:

-- Art Basel Miami Beach

-- Frieze London

-- Art Basel Hong Kong

-- The Armory Show

-- Artissima

-- FIAC

-- SCOPE

-- VOLTA New York

-- Scope Basel

-- The Other Art Fair

Art fairs are typically held over a period of a few days, and they can be a lot of fun. If you're interested in art, you can't miss the opportunity to see a wide variety of art, from paintings and sculptures to photographs and video installations. You'll chat up artists from all over the world and have a chance to interact with super cool people. You can buy the art or just learn about the art and follow the artists.

Art fairs are a must-attend for any art lover. They're a chance to see the latest and greatest in contemporary art, from paintings and sculptures to photographs and video installations. You can also meet and interact with artists from all over the world, and learn about the latest trends in art.

~

A Recital

Recitals are music showcases by people learning music or studying a musical instrument. They are a total vibe for any music lover. They're a chance to see and hear some of the most talented young musicians in the world, performing everything from classical to jazz to pop. You can also show your support for your friends and classmates, and have a night out with your crew.

Here are some of the top recitals in the world:

-- The Juilliard School Recitals

-- The Curtis Institute of Music Recitals

-- The New England Conservatory Recitals

-- The Peabody Institute Recitals

-- The Manhattan School of Music Recitals

Recitals are typically held in concert halls or theaters, and they can last anywhere from an hour to two hours.

When you go to a recital, you can expect to see a variety of performances, including solo, chamber, and orchestral music. You can also expect to hear some amazing music, and to see some of the most talented musicians who are up and coming in the music scene.

Recitals are an important part of the arts and culture sphere. They help to promote the work of young musicians, and to make classical music more accessible to the public. If you're interested in music, we highly recommend checking out a recital near you.

~

A Street Festival

Street festivals are an amazing showcase for cultural celebrations. They're a chance to see and experience a variety of art, music, food, and customs, all in one place. You can also show your support for local businesses and artists, and have a night out with your family and friends.

Here are some of the top street festivals in the world:

-- Notting Hill Carnival in London, England

-- New Orleans Jazz & Heritage Festival in New Orleans, Louisiana

-- Carnaval in Rio de Janeiro, Brazil

-- Day of the Dead in Mexico City, Mexico

-- Holi in India

Street festivals are typically held in public streets or parks, and they can last anywhere from a few hours to a few days. When you go to a street festival, you can expect to see a variety of performances, including music, dance, theater, and art. You can also expect to try a variety of food, and to shop at local vendors.

Street festivals are an important part of the arts and culture scene. They help to promote the work of local artists and businesses, and to make art and culture more accessible to the public. Here are some specific ways to make the most of a street festival:

-- Plan ahead. Check out the festival's website to see what kind of performances and activities will be happening. This will help you decide what to wear and bring with you.

-- Get there early. Street festivals can get crowded, so it's best to get there early to secure a good spot.

-- Be open to new experiences. Street festivals are a great way to try new things and meet new people.

-- Have fun! Street festivals are a great way to let loose and enjoy yourself.

~

A Jazz Festival

Yo, so a jazz festival is like a lit celebration of the smoothest, grooviest music genre out there - jazz, baby! It's a gathering of musicians, artists, and fans who come together to vibe and jam out to some killer tunes. Jazz is one of the most sophisticated and nuanced music genres, so you know these events are cool.

Jazz is a genre of music characterized by improvisation, syncopation, swing, and expressive individuality of musicians. It originated in the United States in the late 19th and early 20th centuries. It emerged from the cultural melting pot of African, European, and Caribbean musical traditions, particularly in the African American communities of New Orleans, Louisiana.

Jazz festivals are a crucial part of the arts and culture scene because they help keep the jazz music legacy alive and kicking. They're a chance for younger peeps to discover and appreciate the classic jazz tunes, and for seasoned jazz cats to showcase their skills and connect with the community.

When you hit up a jazz festival, expect an enchanting experience while you're surrounded by chill people of all ages, dressed to impress in their best jazz-inspired threads (sometimes very flamboyantly!). It's a super cool atmosphere where you can just relax, soak up the vibes and let the music carry you away.

Some of the most prominent and widely attended jazz festivals include the Newport Jazz Festival, the Montreux Jazz Festival, and the New Orleans Jazz & Heritage Festival. These events are renowned for their exceptional programming, world-class performers, and unparalleled atmosphere.

And the best part? Jazz festivals are usually affordable or even free, so you don't need to break the bank to get into the action. Just bring your good vibes, an open mind, and some cash for food and swag, and you're good to go. Overall, jazz festivals are a remarkable celebration of the artistry, creativity, and cultural significance of jazz music, and should be experienced by all who appreciate the finest expressions of human creativity.

~

A Poetry Reading

A poetry reading is an awesome way to experience the magic of language and connect with a community of like-minded people who share a passion for the written word. It's a gathering where poets come together to share their work, often in front of a live audience, and create a space for deep emotional resonance and connection.

Poetry readings are an integral part of the arts and culture world, as they provide a platform for poets to showcase their work, gain exposure, and build a community of like-minded individuals. They also serve to inspire and enrich the literary landscape of our society.

When attending a poetry reading, one can expect to be immersed in a world of lyrical beauty and emotional resonance. The atmosphere is often intimate, with a strong sense of camaraderie and appreciation for the art of poetry. The dress code at a poetry reading is typically casual, but it's always fun to dress the part and show off your personal style. And the best part? Many poetry readings are free or low-cost, so you don't have to break the bank to attend.

Some of the most prominent and widely attended poetry readings include the Dodge Poetry Festival and the National Poetry Slam. These events are renowned for their exceptional programming, world-class poets, and unparalleled atmosphere.

Attending a poetry reading is an incredible opportunity to explore the creative and imaginative forces that drive our world, and to connect with a vibrant community of people who share a love for the power of language.

~

A Book Tour

A book tour is when an author travels and promotes their work, often through readings, signings, and interviews. They're out there to engage with audiences and share their experience writing the book. It's an in-person way to swoon over a new book and the (famous or soon-to-be-famous) author.

Book tours are important to the arts and culture world because they provide a platform for authors to share their work and connect with readers, building a sense of community and fostering a love for literature. They also serve to inspire and enrich the literary landscape of our society. Also, it's great for marketing and PR ;)

Attending a book tour is a unique experience that can vary depending on the author and the event. You can expect to meet a diverse range of people, from fellow book lovers and literary enthusiasts to curious minds who want to learn more about the author and their work.

Most book tours are free, and you don't have to buy the book…but if you do, the author will sign it for you. Already have the book? Bring it along!

Some of the most well-known book tours include those of Michelle Obama, Suzanne Collins, and Stephen King. These events are renowned for their exceptional programming, world-class people watching, and unparalleled atmosphere. Book tours are an incredible way to hobnob with the literati.

~

A Film Festival

A film festival is an exciting and dynamic event that brings together filmmakers, actors, industry professionals, and movie lovers to showcase and celebrate the art of cinema. It's a platform for emerging and established filmmakers to showcase their work, connect with audiences, and gain recognition and exposure.

Film festivals are important to the art world because they promote and celebrate the art of filmmaking. You'll see diverse voices and perspectives. The festivals foster creativity and innovation in the film industry and help to shape the cultural landscape of our society.

Attending a film festival is a thrilling and immersive experience that can vary depending on the festival and the program. You can expect to see a broad range of films, from independent and experimental works to mainstream and popular titles. You may also have the opportunity to attend Q&A sessions with filmmakers and actors, participate in workshops and panels, and socialize with fellow movie lovers.

The dress code at a film festival can vary depending on the event, but it's always a good idea to dress up and show off your personal style. And the best part? Many film festivals offer affordable or even free screenings, but others are closed to the public because they're only for industry professionals.

Some of the most well-known film festivals include the Cannes Film Festival, the Sundance Film Festival, and the Toronto International Film Festival. These events are renowned for their exceptional programming, world-class films, and unparalleled atmosphere.

Overall, attending a film festival is an incredible opportunity to explore the creative and imaginative forces that drive our world, and to connect with a vibrant community of people who share a love for the art of cinema. And yes, you'll see movie stars.

~

Comic Con

Comic Con is an annual celebration of the art, culture, and fandom of comics, movies, TV shows, and other forms of popular media. It's a gathering of artists, creators, fans, and enthusiasts to experience the latest and greatest in pop culture.

Comic Con is important to the art world because it showcases the creativity and imagination of artists and creators, and provides a platform for fans to connect and engage with their favorite content. It's a cultural phenomenon that has helped to shape and define our society's love for pop culture.

Attending Comic Con is an incredible experience that can vary depending on the event and the program. You'll see a wide range of exhibits, panels, and presentations, from exclusive sneak peeks at upcoming movies and TV shows to meet-and-greets with your favorite artists and actors. You may also have the opportunity to participate in cosplay contests, gaming tournaments, and other exciting activities.

The dress code at Comic Con is typically casual, but many attendees choose to dress up in cosplay costumes to show off their favorite characters. And while some Comic Con events can be expensive, many offer affordable or have free admission to certain parts for the public.

Some of the most well-known Comic Con events include San Diego Comic-Con, New York Comic Con, and Emerald City Comic Con. These events are renowned for their exceptional programming, celebrity guests, and unparalleled atmosphere. If you love the DC, Marvel, and comic worlds, definitely put a Comic Con on your list. Go immerse yourself in the world of pop culture, connect with fellow fans, and experience the latest and greatest in art and entertainment.

~

A Language Expo

A language expo is a molto buono event that celebrates the diversity of languages and cultures around the world. It's a platform for language enthusiasts, linguists, and language learners to come together and explore the rich tapestry of human communication.

Language expos are important to the art world because they showcase the beauty and complexity of language, and promote cultural understanding and exchange. They provide a forum for people to share their experiences and knowledge, and to learn from each other in a supportive and inclusive environment.

Attending a language expo is a fascinating experience. You can expect to see a wide range of exhibits and presentations, from language learning resources and materials to cultural displays and performances. You may also have the opportunity to participate in workshops and language exchange sessions, and to meet people from all over the world who share your passion for language.

Language expos are low-cost, but you'll probably have to travel to the good conferences. Some of the most well-known language expos include the Polyglot Conference, the International Linguistics Olympiad, and the Language Show Live. These events are renowned for their exceptional programming, world-class speakers, and unparalleled atmosphere.

Overall, attending a language expo is an incredible opportunity to explore the fascinating world of language and culture, and to connect with a vibrant community of people who share your passion for learning and discovery.

~

Oktoberfest

Oktoberfest is the world's largest Volksfest (beer festival) and is held annually in Munich, Bavaria, Germany. It is a 16-day event running from late September to the first weekend in October where you can party with more than six million of your closest friends from around the world.

Oktoberfest began in 1810 as a wedding celebration for Crown Prince Ludwig of Bavaria and Princess Therese of Saxe-Hildburghausen. The event was a huge success and was repeated the following year. Over time, Oktoberfest has grown into a massive festival that features traditional Bavarian food, music, and beer. Similar events are repeated all over the world.

There are also Oktoberfest celebrations in the US, Canada, & Australia. These festivals typically feature traditional Bavarian food, music, and beer, but they may also include other elements, such as parades, carnival rides, and games. You can drink some of the best beer in the world.

Oktoberfest is an important part of Bavarian culture and is a popular tourist destination.

What goes on at Oktoberfest?

-- Lots of beer: Oktoberfest is a beer festival, so you can expect to find plenty of beer on tap. There are over 6 million liters of beer consumed at Oktoberfest each year!

-- Traditional Bavarian food: Oktoberfest is also a great place to try traditional Bavarian food. Some of the most popular dishes include sausages, roast chicken, and pretzels.

-- Live music: There is live music playing throughout Oktoberfest. You can find traditional Bavarian music, as well as more modern genres.

-- Carnival rides: There are also carnival rides and games at Oktoberfest. This is a great place to try your luck at winning a prize!

-- A sense of community: Oktoberfest is a great place to meet people from all over the world. It is a festive and welcoming atmosphere where everyone can enjoy themselves.

If you are looking for a fun and exciting way to experience Bavarian culture, then Oktoberfest is the perfect event for you. Be sure to book your tickets early, as Oktoberfest is a very popular event!

~

The Amsterdam Tulip Festival

The Amsterdam Tulip Festival is a must-see for any visitor to the Netherlands in the springtime. The festival, running since 1929, takes place every year from late March to early May, and it features millions of tulips in bloom. The tulips are arranged in stunning displays throughout the city, and there are also a variety of events and activities taking place during the festival.

One of the best things about the Amsterdam Tulip Festival is the opportunity to see tulips in their natural habitat. The tulip fields outside of Amsterdam are a sight to behold, and they are the perfect place to take photos or simply enjoy the beauty of nature.

Keukenhof Gardens is the largest flower garden in the world, and it is located just outside of Amsterdam. The gardens are home to millions of tulips, as well as other flowers, such as daffodils, hyacinths, and lilies. There are a variety of flower shows taking place throughout the city during the festival. These shows feature tulips and other flowers, as well as displays of plants and flowers from around the world.

In addition to the tulip fields, the Festival also features a variety of other attractions. There are flower shows, concerts, and other events taking place throughout the city. There are also plenty of opportunities to sample Dutch food and drink, and to shop for souvenirs. It's a truly magical experience. You celebrate spring while enjoying the beauty of the Netherlands.

Admission to the festival is free, but there may be a charge for some of the events and attractions. There is no specific dress code for the festival, but it is generally recommended to wear comfortable clothing and shoes. You will likely meet a variety of people at the festival, including locals, tourists, and other flower lovers.

~

Art Therapy

Art therapy is a form of therapy that uses art to help people express themselves and to cope with stress, anxiety, and other mental health issues. It is a safe and supportive space where people can explore their emotions through art.

Art therapy can be used to address a variety of issues, including trauma, mental health disorders, and physical health conditions. Art therapy can help people who have experienced trauma to process their experiences and to develop coping mechanisms. It can also be used to treat a variety of mental health disorders, including depression, anxiety, and post-traumatic stress disorder. Finally, art therapy can be used to improve physical health conditions, such as chronic pain and cancer, to cope with their symptoms, and to improve their quality of life.

A creative and expressive form of therapy, the arts can be helpful for people of all ages. They are non-threatening and non-judgmental spaces where people can explore their emotions and to develop coping mechanisms under the guidance of a trained professional.

If you are interested in learning more about art therapy, there are a number of resources available online and in your community. You can also talk to your doctor or mental health professional about whether art therapy is right for you.

Here are some of the prominent organizations in the world of art therapy:

-- The **American Art Therapy Association (AATA)** is the largest professional organization for art therapists in the United States. The AATA hosts an annual conference and publishes a variety of resources on art therapy.

-- The **International Association for Art Therapy (IATA)** hosts an international conference every three years and publishes a variety of resources on art therapy.

-- The **National Coalition of Creative Arts Therapies (NCCAT)** is a coalition of organizations that represent the creative arts therapies, including art therapy. The NCCAT advocates for the creative arts therapies and provides resources to the public.

Art therapy is a valuable tool that can help people to express themselves, to cope with stress and anxiety, and to improve their overall well-being. If you are interested in learning more about art therapy, we encourage you to do some research and to talk to your doctor or mental health professional.

~

Arts and Culture Management

Arts and cultural event management is a growing field that encompasses the planning, organizing, and execution of events that promote art and culture. Event managers work with a variety of stakeholders, including artists, performers, venues, and sponsors, to create memorable experiences for audiences.

Event Managers promote culture by introducing people to new forms of art and culture, and can help to foster a sense of community around these shared interests. Cultural events provide educational opportunities and can help to raise awareness of important issues. They also attract visitors to a city and can help to boost local businesses.

The experience of attending an arts or cultural event can be truly transformative. Events can provide a space for people to come together, to be inspired, and to learn. They can also be a lot of fun!

If you are interested in a career in arts and cultural event management, there are a few things you should know. First, you will need to have a strong understanding of art and culture. You should also be organized, detail-oriented, and have excellent communication skills.

Some careers in arts and cultural event management include:

-- Event manager: Event managers are responsible for the overall planning, organization, and execution of events. They work with a variety of stakeholders to ensure that events run smoothly and that guests have a memorable experience.

-- Venue manager: Venue managers are responsible for the day-to-day operations of a venue, such as a theater, concert hall, or museum. They oversee the booking of events, the maintenance of the facility, and the staff.

-- Marketing and promotion manager: Marketing and promotion managers are responsible for creating and executing marketing campaigns for events. They work to generate awareness of events and to encourage people to attend.

-- Fundraising manager: Fundraising managers are responsible for raising money to support arts and cultural events. They work with donors to secure funding and to manage the finances of events.

There are a variety of educational programs available to prepare you for a career in arts and cultural event management. These programs can teach you the skills you need to plan, organize, and execute successful events. Consider a bachelor's degree, master's degree, or certificate program in the field of arts and culture. Also, get involved in your community: volunteer, attend events, and meet people in the field. You could intern with an arts organization or apply to work at a cultural organization. Some entrepreneurs start their own event management business and do quite well! Build your network immediately by attending industry events, connecting with people on social media, and staying up-to-date on trends in the field.

~

Glassblowing

Glassblowing is a centuries-old art form that involves shaping molten glass into objects of beauty and utility. It is a hot and dangerous process, but it can also be incredibly rewarding. Glassblowers use a variety of tools and techniques to create their work, including blowpipes, shears, and paddles. They must be skilled in both hand-eye coordination and precision.

Glassblowing is an important part of the art world. It is used to create everything from sculptures to jewelry to functional objects. Glassblowers often collaborate with other artists, such as painters and sculptors, to create unique and innovative works.

The experience of watching a glassblower work is truly fascinating. It is amazing to see how they can transform a hot, molten blob of glass into something beautiful and intricate. If you have the opportunity to attend a glassblowing demonstration, we highly recommend it. Or you can take a class! Glassblowing classes can range in price from $50 to $500, depending on the length of the class and the materials used.

Here are some of the most famous or biggest events in the world of glassblowing:

-- The Venice Biennale: This international art exhibition is held every two years in Venice, Italy. It is one of the most prestigious art exhibitions in the world, and glassblowing is often featured prominently.

-- The Corning Museum of Glass: This museum in Corning, New York, is home to a world-renowned collection of glass art. It also offers a variety of educational programs and workshops on glassblowing.

-- The Pilchuck Glass School: This school in Stanwood, Washington, is one of the leading glassblowing schools in the world. It offers a variety of programs for both beginners and experienced glassblowers.

Glassblowing is an exciting and challenging art form that has been around for centuries. It is a great way to express your creativity and to create something truly unique. If you are interested in learning more about glassblowing, we encourage you to check out some of the resources listed above.

~

Antiquing

Antiquing is a journey through time! It is the act of searching for and buying antiques, which are items that are at least 100 years old. Antiques can be found in a variety of places, including antique shops, flea markets, and estate sales.

Antiquing is a popular hobby for people of all ages. It can be a great way to find unique and affordable pieces of art, furniture, and other home decor. It can also be a fun way to learn about history and culture.

When antiquing, it is important to be prepared to haggle. The asking price is often not the final price. It is also important to do your research on the items you are interested in. This will help you to avoid overpaying.

You can find unique and affordable pieces of art, furniture, and other home decor if you're savvy! There are some totally famous antiquing events:

-- The Brimfield Antique Show - the largest antique show in the United States. It is held every year in Brimfield, Massachusetts.

-- The New York City Antiques Show - one of the most prestigious antique shows in the world. It is held every year in New York City.

-- Marché aux Puces de Saint-Ouen (The Puces) - the largest flea market in the world and is located in Paris, France. It is a great place to find all sorts of antiques, from furniture to jewelry to art.

-- The European Fine Art Fair (TEFAF) - a four-day event that takes place in Maastricht, Netherlands. It is one of the most prestigious art fairs in the world and is a great place to find all sorts of fine art, including paintings, sculptures, and jewelry.

Antiquing is a great way to find unique and affordable pieces, but also valuable relics from times gone by. If you are looking for a unique and rewarding hobby, antiquing is a great option.

Here are some tips for antiquing:

-- Do your research: Before you go antiquing, it is important to do your research on the items you are interested in. This will help you to avoid overpaying.

-- Be prepared to haggle: The asking price is often not the final price. Be prepared to haggle with the seller to get the best possible price.

-- Dress comfortably: You will be doing a lot of walking when you are antiquing. It is important to dress comfortably so that you can enjoy your time.

-- Be patient: It may take some time to find the perfect piece. Be patient and don't give up.

~

Web Series Festival Global

Web Series Festival Global is an awards festival in Hollywood celebrating the best web series from around the world since 2015. It showcases a wide variety of genres, from comedy to drama to documentary.

Web series are a new and exciting form of art that offers a unique opportunity for creators to tell their stories in a personal and accessible way. Web Series Festival Global promotes web series as a legitimate form of art and provides a platform for creators to connect with and learn from each other.

If you're a fan of web series or are interested in learning more about this new form of art, you should check out Web Series Festival Global. You can see the best web series from around the world and meet other fans and creators. You can expect to watch a variety of web series, meet other fans and creators, learn about the latest trends, and network with professionals in the industry. Web Series Festival Global is an affordable event that regularly offers day passes for around $20 and weekend passes for $50. The dress code is casual, but you may want to dress to impress if you plan to attend any networking events. Expect to meet creators, producers, and distributors and learn about their work or discuss potential collaborations.

Web Series Festival Global is a wild ride. Are you a content creator? Series fan? New media aficionado? Hollywood guru? Well, you gotta go. Not in Hollywood? Try the NY, Austin, LA, Miami, or Seattle Web Fests.

~

The New York Book Festival

The New York Book Festival is a literary playground for the cool kids. It's an annual event that celebrates the best in contemporary literature. The festival features a wide variety of authors, from established literary heavyweights to up-and-coming indie darlings.

The festival is important to the arts and culture scene in New York City because it provides a platform for emerging writers to share their work with a wider audience. The festival also helps to promote literacy and a love of reading in the city.

The experience of attending the New York Book Festival is unlike anything else. You'll get to meet your favorite authors, hear them speak about their work, and ask them questions. You'll also get to discover new authors and genres that you might not have otherwise known about.

Here's what to expect when you attend the New York Book Festival:

-- Author readings: This is the main event of the festival. You'll get to hear your favorite authors read from their work.

-- Panel discussions: There will be panels on a variety of topics, from writing craft to the future of publishing.

-- Book signings: After the readings and panels, you'll have the chance to meet the authors and get their books signed.

-- Partying: The festival is a great place to let loose and have some fun. There will be parties happening all over the city, so you can dance the night away.

The New York Book Festival is a great way to celebrate the art of literature. It's a fun, inclusive event that's open to everyone. So, if you're a book lover, be sure to check it out. The festival is generally affordable, with tickets starting at around $20. The dress code is casual.

Some of the most famous or biggest events that have been featured at the New York Book Festival include:

-- A conversation between Toni Morrison and Jonathan Safran Foer

-- A panel discussion with Michael Chabon, Jonathan Lethem, and Jeffrey Eugenides

-- A book signing with Margaret Atwood

The New York Book Festival is a great place to discover new books, meet your favorite authors, and celebrate the art of literature. So, if you're a book lover, be sure to check it out.

~

The Global Dance Open

The Global Dance Open is an annual event that celebrates the best in dance from around the world. The festival features a wide variety of styles, from hip-hop to ballet to contemporary. It's important to the arts and culture scene because it provides a platform for emerging dancers to share their work with a wider audience. The festival also helps to promote dance and a love of movement in the community.

The experience of attending the Global Dance Open is spectacular. Dance performances are the main event of the festival. You'll get to see some of the best dancers in the world perform. There are workshops and classes on a variety of topics, from technique to choreography. There's also a ton of social events. Parties and meetups happen all over the city, so you can let loose and have some fun.

The Global Dance Open is a great way to celebrate the art of dance. It's a fun, inclusive event that's open to everyone. So if you're a dancer, or if you just love to dance, be sure to check it out. It's generally affordable, with tickets starting at around $20. The dress code is casual.

If you've been in the past, you might have seen a performance by the Alvin Ailey American Dance Theater, a workshop with choreographer Twyla Tharp, or attended a party with DJ Jazzy Jeff.

The Global Dance Open is a great place to discover new dance styles, meet your favorite dancers, and celebrate the art of dance. So, if you're a dancer, or if you just love to dance, be sure to check it out.

~

The European Wood Sculpture Competition

The European Wood Sculpture Competition is an annual event that brings together chainsaw carvers from all over

Europe since 1992 to compete for the title of best chainsaw carver. The extravaganza is held in a different location each year, and you might have seen it in Oslo, Copenhagen, Zurich, Salzburg, or Munich.

The experience of attending the European Wood Sculpture Competition is unlike anything else. You'll get to see some of the best chainsaw carvers in the world in action, and you'll also get to see the sculptures as they are being created. You'll also get to meet other chainsaw carvers and learn about their work.

You can expect to see a lot of chainsaw carving. It's the main event of the competition. These are the best chainsaw carvers in the world- in action- right in front of you. The sculptures created by the chainsaw carvers are displayed in a public park or other outdoor space, and you can meet the carvers and ask about their work.

The competition is generally affordable, with tickets starting at around $20. It's an inclusive event open to everyone. Some of the most famous or biggest events that have been featured at the European Wood Sculpture Competition include:

-- A sculpture of a giant tree by chainsaw carver Thomas Klepel

-- A sculpture of a family of bears by chainsaw carver Vlad Carving

-- A sculpture of a dragon by chainsaw carver Peter Aicher

The competition is open to all chainsaw carvers, regardless of their age, experience, or nationality. To enter, carvers must submit an application and a portfolio of their work. A panel of judges selects the top 10 carvers to compete in the final round. In the final round, each carver has 24 hours to create a sculpture from a large block of wood. The sculptures are judged on their creativity, technical skill, and overall impact. The winner is announced at the end of the competition. It's a great opportunity for chainsaw carvers to showcase their skills and to compete for a prestigious prize. It is also a great opportunity for the public to see the art of wood carving up close.

~

Winterlude

Winterlude is an annual winter festival held in Ottawa, Canada. It is a celebration of winter featuring a variety of activities, including skating, snowshoeing, ice carving, and concerts. This jam is cool because you've got art, winter sports, and activities.

Seriously, it sounds frigid but it's a must-do for you outdoor lovers. You'll get to party in a winter wonderland, but also be a part of an important arts festival. You'll meet other people who love winter while making frosty new friends.

Considering all the fabulous activities at Winterlude, don't miss:

-- Skating: The Rideau Canal Skateway is a UNESCO World Heritage Site, and it is one of the most popular attractions at Winterlude. You can skate for free on the canal, and there are also guided tours available.

-- Snowshoeing: There are several snowshoe trails in the area, and they offer stunning views of the city. You can rent snowshoes at several locations, and there are also guided tours available.

-- Ice carving: There are several ice carving competitions throughout the festival, and you can watch the artists work their magic. There are also several ice sculptures on display, and you can take photos of them.

-- Concerts: There are several concerts throughout the festival, and they feature a variety of musical genres. You can find concerts at several venues, including the Canadian Parliament Buildings and the Fairmont Chateau Laurier.

-- The Bed Race: This is a hilarious event where teams race beds down the Rideau Canal.

-- The Waiters and Waitresses on Ice Challenge: This is a challenging event where waiters and waitresses race on ice skates while carrying trays of food and drinks.

-- The Snowflake Kingdom: This is a giant snow playground with slides, tunnels, and other structures.

Winterlude is a great way to experience winter in Ottawa. It is a fun, festive atmosphere that's affordable at around $20. The dress code is casual, but dude, dress warm if you plan on doing any outdoor activities. Winterlude is a great place to experience winter in Ottawa. This is a phenomenal opportunity for the perfect selfie, reel, and story. Don't get FOMO- see you in Canada this winter.

~

The International Make-Up Artist Trade Show

The International Make-Up Artist Trade Show (IMATS) is the world's largest makeup trade show, and it's a must-attend event for anyone interested in makeup artistry. The show features hundreds of exhibitors, from major beauty brands to indie companies, all showcasing their latest products and trends.

IMATS is also a great place to learn from the best in the business. There are workshops, demonstrations, and panels on everything from makeup application to special effects. You can also meet your favorite makeup artists and get their autographs. It's a chance to be inspired, learn, and network with other makeup artists from all over the world. If you're serious about makeup artistry, we'll see you at IMATS in LA, NY, Toronto, or London. FYI, it's around $20, and please- dress like the artist you are.

Here's what to expect:

-- Exhibitions: Hundreds of exhibitors will be showcasing their latest products and trends.

-- Workshops: Learn from the best in the business in hands-on workshops.

-- Demonstrations: Watch makeup artists create stunning looks live.

-- Panels: Learn about the latest trends and techniques in makeup artistry.

-- Meet & greets: Meet your favorite makeup artists and get their autographs.

Some of the most famous or biggest events that have been featured at IMATS include:

-- The Battle of the Brushes: This is a competition where makeup students compete to create the best look.

-- The IMATS Pro Awards: These awards recognize the best makeup artists in the industry.

-- The IMATS BeautyCon: This is a festival where people can learn about beauty and fashion.

IMATS is held all over the world several times a year. If you're serious about makeup artistry, IMATS is a must-attend event, at least for Pat McGrath, Kevyn Aucoin, James Charles, and Nikkie Tutorials…if we MUST name drop. Trust us, it's the ultimate makeup experience!

~

A Wine Tour

A wine tour is an experience where you visit different wineries and vineyards to learn about the process of making wine. It is a popular activity in the art world because wine is often associated with sophistication and culture. Wine tours are important to culture because they provide an opportunity to learn about the history and tradition of winemaking, which is an art form in itself.

When you attend a wine tour, you can expect to taste different types of wine, learn about the different grapes used in winemaking, and see the process of how wine is made. The societal context of a wine tour is often one of relaxation and enjoyment, as people come together to appreciate the art of winemaking.

The history of wine tours dates back to ancient times, when wine was considered a luxury item. Today, wine tours can be expensive, but they are often worth the cost for the experience and knowledge gained. People from all walks of life attend wine tours, from casual wine enthusiasts to serious collectors.

The dress code for a wine tour is typically casual, but it depends on the winery. It is important to wear comfortable shoes as you may be walking through vineyards, gravel roads, or up and down stairs. Some of the most famous wine tours include the Napa Valley Wine Train in California, the Bordeaux Wine Tour in France, and the Tuscany Wine Tour in Italy.

Overall, a wine tour is a unique and educational experience that allows you to appreciate the art of winemaking and the culture surrounding it.

~

Salon Du Chocolat

Salon du Chocolat is an annual event that celebrates the art of chocolate making and its cultural significance. It is an important event for the arts and culture community, as it showcases the creativity and skill of chocolatiers from around the world. The experience is a sensory delight, with attendees able to taste and sample a wide variety of chocolate creations.

There's a diverse crowd of people, including chocolatiers, pastry chefs, foodies, and chocolate enthusiasts. The dress code is typically casual, but some attendees really dress up for the occasion.

The history of Salon du Chocolat dates back to 1994, when it was first held in Paris. Since then, it has grown to become one of the largest chocolate events in the world, with events held in cities such as New York, Tokyo, and Moscow. Don't Miss:

-- Chocolate Exhibitions: The Salon du Chocolat showcases a wide range of chocolate-related exhibits, including intricate chocolate sculptures, art installations, and displays of various chocolate products. It offers a visual feast for attendees.

-- Chocolate Tastings: Visitors have the opportunity to sample a diverse selection of chocolates from different regions and chocolatiers. It's a chance to discover unique flavors, textures, and techniques.

-- Chocolate Fashion Shows: One of the highlights of the event is the chocolate-themed fashion shows, where designers create stunning outfits using chocolate as a medium. These edible fashion creations are truly impressive and demonstrate the creativity and versatility of chocolate.

-- Workshops and Demonstrations: The Salon du Chocolat often hosts workshops and demonstrations conducted by renowned chocolatiers, pastry chefs, and experts. Attendees can learn about chocolate-making techniques, participate in tastings, and gain insights into the art of working with chocolate.

-- **Chocolate Market:** The event usually features a chocolate market where visitors can purchase a wide range of chocolate products, including artisanal chocolates, truffles, bars, cocoa beans, and more. It's a great opportunity to explore and buy unique and high-quality chocolates.

The cost of attending Salon du Chocolat varies depending on the location and the type of ticket purchased. However, it is generally considered to be a high-end event, with prices ranging from $20 to $50 per ticket.

Some of the most famous events at Salon du Chocolat include chocolate fashion shows, where models wear clothing made entirely out of chocolate, and chocolate sculpture competitions, where artists create intricate sculptures out of chocolate.

Salon du Chocolat is a must-attend event for anyone who loves chocolate and appreciates the artistry and creativity that goes into making it.

~

The Cherry Blossom Festival

The cherry blossom festival is an annual event that celebrates the blooming of cherry blossom trees. It is a significant event in the art world because it inspires artists to create works of art that capture the beauty of the blossoms.

When you attend the cherry blossom festival, you can expect to see a sea of pink and white blossoms, as well as various cultural performances and activities. The experience is breathtaking, and it is a great opportunity to take photos and enjoy the outdoors.

The festival has a rich history that dates back to ancient Japan, where cherry blossom trees were seen as a symbol of renewal and the fleeting nature of life. Today, the festival is celebrated all over the world, with some of the most famous events taking place in Japan, Washington D.C., and Vancouver.

The cost of attending the festival varies depending on the location and the events you choose to attend. However, many events are free and open to the public.

People from all walks of life attend the festival, including families, couples, and tourists. They will be enjoying the various cultural performances, taking photos, and enjoying the beauty of the blossoms.

There is no specific dress code for the festival, but it is recommended to wear comfortable clothing and shoes for walking around. Some of the biggest events include the National Cherry Blossom Festival in Washington D.C., the Sakura Matsuri Festival in Brooklyn, and the Vancouver Cherry Blossom Festival.

Overall, the cherry blossom festival is a beautiful and culturally significant event that is worth experiencing at least once in your lifetime.

~

The Bay to Breakers

Bay to Breakers is a 12K race that takes place in San Francisco every year. It's a unique event that combines athleticism, creativity, and culture. The race is known for its wild costumes, which range from superheroes to animals to political figures. It's a celebration of individuality and creativity, and it attracts people from all walks of life.

The race has a long history, dating back to 1912. It was originally created as a way to boost morale after the devastating earthquake that hit San Francisco in 1906. Over the years, it has become a beloved tradition in the city, and it's now one of the biggest events of the year.

Bay to Breakers is important to the arts and culture scene in San Francisco because it's a platform for self-expression and creativity. The costumes and floats that people create are works of art in themselves, and they reflect the unique spirit of the city. The race also attracts a diverse crowd, which adds to the cultural richness of the event.

If you attend Bay to Breakers, you can expect a lively and energetic atmosphere. The race starts in downtown San Francisco and winds its way through the city, ending at Ocean Beach. Along the way, you'll see thousands of people in costumes, dancing, and having a good time. There are also plenty of food and drink vendors, as well as live music and entertainment.

The dress code for Bay to Breakers is anything goes. People wear everything from tutus to full-body animal costumes to political satire outfits. The only rule is that you have to wear something, so don't be afraid to get creative.

Some of the most famous events at Bay to Breakers include the centipede race, where teams of runners are connected by a long rope, and the "Bay to Breakers" footrace, which is a race within the race for the fastest runners.

Overall, Bay to Breakers is a unique and exciting event that celebrates the creativity and diversity of San Francisco. It's a must-see for anyone who loves art, culture, and a good time.

~

The Gilroy Garlic Festival

The Gilroy Garlic Festival is an annual event that celebrates all things garlic in Gilroy, California USA. It's a popular festival that draws in people from all over the world. The festival is important to arts and culture because it combines the creativity and talent of local artists and musicians with food.

The experience is like no other, with the smell of garlic filling the air and the sound of live music in the background. When you attend, you can expect to see a variety of garlic-themed foods, such as garlic ice cream and garlic bread. The societal context of the festival is one of community and celebration.

The festival has a rich history, dating back to 1979, and has grown in popularity over the years. The tickets to the festival typically cost around $20. People from all walks of life attend the festival, from families with young children to older adults. The dress code is casual, with many people wearing garlic-themed clothing or accessories. Some of the most famous events at the festival include the garlic cook-off and the garlic braiding contest. Overall, the Gilroy Garlic Festival is a fun and unique event that celebrates the power of garlic and the creativity of local artists and musicians.

~

An Art Auction

An art auction is a public sale of artwork where buyers bid on pieces of art. It is an important event in the art world because it allows artists to showcase their work and collectors to acquire new pieces for their collections. Additionally, due to the money exchanged, this is an important part of the financial art world.

Attending an art auction can be a thrilling experience, as the bidding can become intense and the prices can soar. The societal context of an art auction is often one of luxury and exclusivity, as often only those with the means to bid on expensive artwork are able to attend.

The history of art auctions dates back to the 17th century, when they were first held in London. The cost of attending an art auction can vary greatly, depending on the artwork being sold and the level of interest from buyers.

The dress code for an art auction is typically formal or semi-formal, as it is a high-end event. Some of the most famous art auctions include the Christie's and Sotheby's auctions, which are known for selling some of the most expensive artwork in the world.

At an art auction, you can expect to see a variety of people, including collectors, art enthusiasts, and wealthy individuals. They will be bidding on artwork and discussing the pieces with each other.

~

The World Architecture Festival

The World Architecture Festival is an annual event that brings together architects, designers, and industry professionals from around the world to showcase their work and exchange ideas.

The location varies each year. It's an important event for the arts and culture community because it highlights the latest trends and innovations in architecture and design.

The experience of attending the festival is both educational and inspiring, with a variety of seminars, workshops, and exhibitions to explore. Expect to see some of the most talented and creative minds in the industry, as well as representatives from leading architecture firms and design companies.

The dress code is typically business casual, but some events may require more formal attire.

The festival is not cheap, but it's worth the investment for anyone interested in architecture and design.

Some of the biggest events at the festival include the awards ceremony, where the best projects and designs are recognized, and the keynote speeches from industry leaders.

Overall, the World Architecture Festival is a must-attend event for anyone passionate about architecture and design.

~

An Estate Sale

Sometimes confused with (or purposely mislabeled) a garage sale, an estate sale is a sale of personal property, including artwork, that takes place after someone has passed away or is downsizing their collection. It is important to the art world because it provides an opportunity for collectors and enthusiasts to acquire unique and rare pieces.

The experience of attending an estate sale can be exciting and overwhelming, as there are often many items to browse through and bid on. The societal context of estate sales is often tied to the idea of legacy and passing on possessions to the next generation.

The history of estate sales dates back to ancient times, where the possessions of the deceased were often sold to pay for their funeral expenses. The cost of items at an estate sale can vary greatly, depending on the rarity and condition of the artwork.

People from all walks of life attend estate sales, from serious collectors to casual shoppers looking for a unique piece. There is no dress code for attending an estate sale, but comfortable clothing and shoes are recommended. Some of the most famous estate sales include those of celebrities and historical figures, such as Marilyn Monroe and Jacqueline Kennedy Onassis.

~

A Writer's Retreat

A writer's retreat is a gathering of writers who come together to work on their craft in a supportive and inspiring environment. It's an important part of the arts and culture world because it allows writers to connect with each other, share ideas, and learn from one another.

The experience of attending a writer's retreat can vary depending on the location and the specific retreat, but generally, attendees can expect to have access to workshops, lectures, and one-on-one sessions with experienced writers, coaches, or editors.

A writer's retreat can be a great place to get collaborative brainstorming sessions with other writers, get constructive criticism on your work, and immerse yourself in your craft.

The societal context of a writer's retreat is one of creativity, collaboration, and community. The history of writers' retreats dates back to the early 20th century, when writers began gathering in remote locations to focus on their work.

The cost of attending a writer's retreat can vary widely, depending on the location, the length of the retreat, and the amenities provided.

Dress code is usually casual and comfortable, as the focus is on writing rather than fashion. Some of the most famous writer's retreats include the Bread Loaf Writers' Conference and the Iowa Writers' Workshop.

~

An Artist Colony

An artist colony is a community of artists who live and work together in a shared space. It is important to arts and culture because it provides a supportive environment for artists to create and collaborate.

The experience of attending an artist colony can vary depending on the specific community, but generally, visitors can expect to see a variety of artwork and meet artists from different backgrounds.

The societal context of artist colonies is often one of experimentation and innovation, as artists are encouraged to push boundaries and explore new ideas.

The history of artist colonies dates back to the 19th century, when groups of artists began to gather in rural areas to escape the pressures of urban life.

The cost of attending an artist colony can vary, but many offer scholarships or other forms of financial assistance. People attending an artist colony can expect to see a diverse group of artists working in a variety of mediums, from painting to sculpture to performance art.

There is no specific dress code for attending an artist colony, but comfortable clothing is recommended. Some of the most famous artist colonies include the MacDowell Colony in New Hampshire and the Yaddo Colony in New York.

~

An Art Foundation

An art foundation is a non-profit organization that supports and promotes the arts. It is important to arts and culture because it provides funding for artists and art institutions, as well as educational programs and exhibitions. It provides funding, resources, and opportunities for artists and art organizations to create and showcase their work. The foundation also plays a crucial role in preserving and promoting cultural heritage and diversity.

Attending an art foundation event can be a great way to experience different forms of art, meet artists and art enthusiasts, and learn about the latest trends and developments in the art world. Some of the most famous art foundations include the Guggenheim Foundation, the Getty Foundation, and the Andy Warhol Foundation. These foundations organize various events and exhibitions throughout the year, showcasing the work of both established and emerging artists.

The societal context of art foundations is that they often serve as a bridge between the art world and the general public, helping to make art more accessible to everyone. The history of art foundations dates back to the early 20th century, when wealthy individuals began to establish foundations to support the arts. The cost of attending an art foundation event can vary, but many events are free or have a low admission fee. People from all walks of life can attend art foundation events, from artists and collectors to students and casual art lovers. The dress code for art foundation events is typically business casual or smart casual.

~

An Artist Residency

An artist residency program is a period of time during which an artist is given the opportunity to live and work in a supportive environment. These programs can be found all over the world, and they offer a variety of benefits to artists, including time to focus on their work without distractions, access to resources and equipment, opportunities to meet other artists and collaborate, and a chance to get feedback on their work.

Artist residency programs have a long history, dating back to the 17th century. Some of the most famous artist residencies include the Yaddo Artists Colony in New York, the MacDowell Colony in New Hampshire, and the Bellagio Center in Italy.

These important programs provide artists with the opportunity to grow and develop their work. They also help to foster a sense of community among artists and to promote creativity.

What does an artist do during an artist residency program?

-- Create new artwork

-- **Experiment with new techniques**

-- **Collaborate with other artists**

-- **Give presentations or workshops**

-- **Attend lectures or workshops**

-- **Take advantage of the resident community**

Artist residency programs are a great way for artists to get ahead in their careers. They offer a unique opportunity to focus on your work, collaborate with other artists, and learn from experts. If you are an artist, we encourage you to research artist residency programs in your area and apply for one. Some are programs you pay for, while others offer grants and scholarships.

~

A Sound Bath

A sound bath is a type of meditation that uses sound to create a state of relaxation and well-being. The sound is created by a variety of instruments, including gongs, singing bowls, and tuning forks. The participants lie or sit comfortably and listen to the sound, which is often accompanied by guided imagery or music.

Sound baths have been shown to have a number of benefits, including:

-- **Reduced stress and anxiety**

-- **Improved sleep**

-- Increased relaxation

-- Enhanced creativity

-- Improved focus and concentration

Sound baths are a safe and enjoyable way to relax and de-stress. They are also a great way to connect with your inner self and to experience the healing power of sound.

If you are interested in trying a sound bath, there are many places where you can find them. You can search online or ask your local yoga studio or meditation center if they offer sound baths.

Here are some additional details about sound baths:

-- Sound baths are often held in a darkened room, which helps to create a sense of peace and tranquility.

-- The participants are usually asked to lie down on the floor or sit in a comfortable chair.

-- The sound therapist will often play a variety of instruments, including gongs, singing bowls, and tuning forks.

-- The participants are encouraged to close their eyes and relax.

-- The sound therapist may lead the participants through a guided meditation or simply allow them to listen to the sound.

-- Sound baths typically last for about an hour.

Sound baths can be a very relaxing and beneficial experience. If you are looking for a way to reduce stress, improve your sleep, or simply relax, definitely try a sound bath.

~

Burning Man

Burning Man is a week-long art festival held in the Black Rock Desert in Nevada every year. It started in 1986 as a small gathering of friends and has since grown into a massive event with over 70,000 attendees. Burning Man is a unique experience that celebrates creativity, self-expression, and community. There are no rules or restrictions at Burning Man, and everyone is encouraged to let loose and have fun. It's a carry-in, carry-out, zero footprint event.

The Burning Man festival is important for arts and culture because it provides a platform for artists to showcase their work. There are no commercial sponsors at Burning Man, so all of the art is created by the attendees. This creates a unique and vibrant art scene that is unlike anything else in the world. See the mutant vehicles, the dust celebrations, and the pure joy of community.

The Burning Man festival also represents the idea of radical self-expression. Everyone is free to be themselves, regardless of their age, race, gender, or social status. This creates a welcoming and inclusive environment.

There are 10 principles of Burning Man:

*Radical Inclusion

*Gifting

*Decommodification

*Radical Self-reliance

*Radical Self-expression

*Communal Effort

*Civic Responsibility

*Leaving No Trace

*Participation

*Immediacy

This is what you do during Burning Man:

-- Explore the art: Burning Man is home to some of the most incredible art in the world. There are giant sculptures, interactive art installations, and even entire art cities to explore.

-- Dance all night long: Burning Man is a party, and there's always music playing somewhere. Whether you're into electronic music, techno, or something else entirely, you're sure to find a dance party that you'll love.

-- Create your own art: Burning Man is a place where you can let your creativity run wild. There are workshops, classes, and even entire camps dedicated to helping you create your own art.

-- Meet new people: Burning Man is a great place to meet new people from all over the world. Everyone is friendly and welcoming, and there's no pressure to be anything other than yourself.

-- Give back to the community: Burning Man is a community-oriented event, and there are many ways to give back. You can volunteer your time, donate to the Burning Man Project, or even create your own project to help others.

~

Coachella

Coachella Valley Music and Arts Festival is an annual two-weekend music and arts festival held at the Empire Polo Club in Indio, California. The festival features many genres of music, including rock, pop, electronic dance music, hip hop, and country, as well as art installations, performances, and other activities.

Coachella was founded in 1999 by Paul Tollett and Rick Alverson. The first festival was held on October 12–14, 1999, and featured Beck, Morrissey, The Chemical Brothers, and The Prodigy. The festival was a success, and it has since grown into one of the largest and most popular music festivals in the world. Not sure where to start at Coachella? Follow us!

-- Hear the music: Coachella features a wide variety of music, so you're sure to find something you'll love. Headliners in 2023 include Harry Styles, Billie Eilish, and Doja Cat.

-- **Explore the art:** Coachella is also known for its art installations. There are large-scale sculptures, interactive exhibits, and even a few art cars that you can explore.

-- **Dress up:** Coachella is a great place to let your creativity run wild. There are no dress codes, so you can wear whatever you want. Many people choose to dress up in elaborate costumes.

-- **Dance all day and night:** Coachella is a party, and there's always music playing somewhere. Whether you're into electronic music, hip hop, or something else entirely, you're sure to find a dance party that you'll love.

-- **Meet new people:** Coachella is a great place to meet new people from all over the world. Everyone is friendly and welcoming, and there's no pressure to be anything other than yourself.

-- **Camp out:** Coachella is a camping festival, so you'll need to bring your own gear. This can be a great way to save money and get a more immersive experience.

-- **Take a day trip:** If you're feeling adventurous, take a day trip to one of the many nearby attractions, like the Palm Springs Aerial Tramway, Joshua Tree National Park, or the Salton Sea.

~

Recycled Art

Recycled art is a type of art that uses recycled materials, such as old furniture, bottles, cans, and other discarded items. It is a growing trend in the art world, and there are many talented artists who are creating beautiful and unique works of art from recycled materials.

The first recycled art museum was founded in 1994 in the Netherlands. There are many online communities dedicated to recycled art.

Some of the most well-known works of recycled art include:

-- The Trash People by Jason deCaires Taylor: These sculptures are made from recycled plastic and are located on the ocean floor in the Bahamas.

-- The Recycled City by Vik Muniz: This series of photographs depicts famous landmarks made from recycled materials, such as the Statue of Liberty made from sugar cubes and the Sistine Chapel made from chewing gum.

-- The Upcycled Fashion Show by Trash is for Tossers: This fashion show features clothes made from recycled materials, such as plastic bags, soda cans, and old tires.

The best appreciation for recycled art is found in:

-- The United Kingdom: The UK has a strong tradition of recycling, and there are many museums and galleries that showcase recycled art.

-- The Netherlands: The Netherlands is also a very environmentally conscious country, and there are many festivals and events that celebrate recycled art.

-- The United States: The US has a growing interest in recycled art, and there are many artists and organizations working to promote this type of art.

Recycled art dates back to the early 20th century. Artists such as Marcel Duchamp and Pablo Picasso began to experiment with using found objects in their work. In the 1960s, the environmental movement led to a renewed interest in recycled art. In the 1990s, the rise of the internet and social media helped to popularize recycled art around the world.

This is a growing trend that is making a positive impact on the environment and the arts. It provides a new way to create art that is both beautiful and environmentally friendly. It inspires people to think about the environment and how they can reduce their impact on the planet. It's a unique and creative way to express oneself, and it is a powerful way to raise awareness of waste, recycling, and environmental issues.

~

The International Garden Festival

The International Garden Festival is a world-renowned event that showcases the best in contemporary garden design. It is held every two years in Chaumont-sur-Loire, France, and attracts visitors from all over the world.

The festival was founded in 1992 by Jacques Grange, a French landscape architect. The first festival was a small event, but it quickly grew in popularity. Today, the festival is a major cultural event that features over 30 gardens created by some of the world's leading garden designers.

The festival is important to arts and culture because it celebrates the beauty and diversity of garden design. It also provides a platform for new and emerging designers to showcase their work. The festival has been attended by many famous people, including Princess Diana, David Hockney, and Mick Jagger.

Some of the best works and gardeners / artists at the International Garden Festival include:

-- The Water Garden by Piet Oudolf: This garden is a beautiful and serene oasis that features a variety of water features.

-- The Bamboo Garden by Patrick Blanc: This garden is a vertical garden that features over 100 species of bamboo.

-- The Sensory Garden by Gilles Clément: This garden is designed to stimulate all of the senses.

The International Garden Festival is a must-see for anyone interested in garden design, landscape architecture, or art. It is a beautiful and inspiring event that celebrates the beauty of nature. It is important to arts and culture because it provides a platform for people to learn about different cultures and traditions through the lens of gardening. It encourages creativity and innovation in garden design. It promotes sustainability and environmental awareness, and it's a place where people come together to celebrate nature.

~

A Shakespeare Festival

A Shakespeare festival is an event that celebrates the works of William Shakespeare through performances, workshops, and other activities. It is important to arts and culture because it allows people to experience and appreciate the timeless beauty of Shakespeare's plays.

The experience of attending a Shakespeare festival can be both educational and entertaining, with opportunities to learn about the history and context of the plays, as well as to see them performed by talented actors. Oftentimes, the classic plays are set in different time periods or situations while maintaining the same plot.

The societal context of a Shakespeare festival is one of celebration and appreciation for the arts, and the history of these festivals dates back to the 19th century.

The cost of attending a Shakespeare festival can vary depending on the location and the events offered, but many festivals offer free or low-cost options, especially if you look for tickets well in advance. People of all ages and backgrounds can attend a Shakespeare festival, and the dress code is typically casual.

Some of the most famous Shakespeare festivals include the Stratford Festival in Canada and the Shakespeare Festival in Ashland, Oregon.

~

Blue Chip Art

Blue chip art is like the rock stars of the art world, my friend. We're talking about those jaw-dropping, mind-blowing artworks that everyone drools over. It's like the cream of the crop, the best of the best. These pieces are created by super famous artists who have left their mark on art history. And let me tell you, they hold major street cred in the arts and culture scene.

When you step into a blue chip art event, get ready for an experience that's out of this world. Picture yourself surrounded by a crowd of art fanatics, collectors, curators, and even the artists themselves. They'll be geeking out, having heated discussions about art, and sharing their philosophical insights. And hey, dress to impress- we're talking elegant and classy vibes.

Now, here's the deal with blue chip art. It's not just about how insanely awesome it looks (although that's a big part). It's also about the big bucks it fetches. We're talking crazy expensive prices that make your head spin. These artworks can make it rain at auctions and private sales, attracting some serious high rollers.

Let me drop some names on you. Art Basel, Frieze Art Fair, and the Venice Biennale are the hottest events in the blue chip art world. It's where the who's who of the art scene gather to show off their coolest creations, strike deals, and soak up the creative vibes. These events shape the direction of contemporary art.

Blue chip art is where creativity meets fame and fortune.

~

CHAPTER 7 ✿ Do I Sound Like I Know What I'm Talking About?

Welcome, intrepid art enthusiasts, to the thrilling end to your journey through the vast and captivating world of the arts!

In this chapter, we embark on an exhilarating quest to test your knowledge and uncover the hidden gems of art history, the intricacies of art vocabulary, the pulse of arts and culture events, and the latest buzz in the ever-evolving art world.

But hey, you, brilliant reader, might be wondering if you even need to take a quiz. Fear not, for we assure you, this quiz is not your average run-of-the-mill examination. It's a delightfully engaging multiple-choice challenge featuring art-centric brain teasers pulled directly from this book. This quiz will both entertain and enlighten you. You dove deep into the heart of creativity and culture, so you probably already know all the answers. Probably. We hope. Anyway, good luck.

As you delve into this whimsical quiz, prepare to be mesmerized by your astonishing knowledge of artists past, dazzled by your diverse and colorful palette of art terminology, and swept off your feet by the enchanting allure of your plans to attend the most exciting arts and culture events worldwide. You'll find yourself unearthing hidden knowledge like an art detective on a thrilling quest. So, fasten your seatbelts, and let's see the brilliance that lies within you!

~

We got **questions**. You got **answers**?

(**Fine, we'll** give y**ou the** ans**wers**. The**y're** in CHAP**TER** 8.)

~

1. **Why** are the **arts** impo**rtant for ever**yone?

    A. They foster **empa**thy and **underst**anding

    B. They enhance **communi**cation and **expre**ssion

    C. They stimulate **crit**ical **think**ing

    D. All of the above

2. **Why** are **arts** and **cult**ure **impo**rtant for **diver**sity?

    A. The arts **celeb**rate and **prom**ote **divers**ity and are **a cata**lyst for **cult**ural **progre**ssion

    B. Because my art teacher **said so**

    C. There's a lot of art on political posters

    D. I saw **a dog paint once in a YouT**ube **video**

3. What was the dawn of art? We're talking history from waaaaaaay back!

    A. Probably Greek and Roman times. Or Egypt. Maybe Mayan?

    B. Prehistoric times, when our ancestors left their mark on cave walls with paintings and handprints

    C. Nothing was real before the internet

    D. Whenever Leonardo Da Vinci was doing his thing

4. What is the digital art revolution?

    A. When you Venmo someone your share of the cinema tickets

    B. Y2K art

    C. A movement that's driving contemporary art, aided by advances in VR and AR to blur the boundaries between the real and the virtual art worlds

    D. Something to do with using bitcoins to buy art

5. Why are we exploring space art?

   A. Because of the US creating a space force

   B. All the news about aliens got us thinking about art

   C. We ran out of things on Earth to make art about

   D. Because celestial wonders and challenges of interplanetary exploration inspire us and we're experimenting with new art techniques for our future interplanetary habitats.

6. What is bioart?

   A. The art of biotechnology to explore the convergence of art and science

   B. Using flowers to make art

   C. Using soil and dirt to make art

   D. Art made on farms

7. What is neuroart?

A. The name for new art being made now

B. Art made by first year psychology students

C. Art made measuring waves in the ocean

D. Art created with and / or inspired by technology measuring neural activity

8. Why is there so much religion in arts and culture?

A. Religious beliefs are expressed through cultural rituals and traditions

B. We only do watercolor classes on holy days

C. Religious leaders love art

D. Each culture has super artistic deities

9. Why are **freeports** so **secre**tive?

    A. They have crazy high-security, they're always in spy movies, and they have different and confusing legal regulations, making them defacto tax havens

    B. Because they are soooo boring

    C. That's where they keep the aliens

    D. Because keeping secrets is fun

10. What is cultural repatriation?

    A. France returning cultural and historical artifacts to Africa

    B. Countries / Individuals returning cultural and historical artifacts to the countries / nations / people the items were taken from

    C. England returning cultural and historical artifacts to Nigeria

    D. All of the above

11. Why is cultural heritage at risk?

A. Everything is pirated on the internet now

B. Everyone is on their phones all the time

C. Climate change, urbanization, and conflict pose existential threats to countless cultural landmarks

D. It is not

12. What are some good ways to preserve art for the future?

A. Conserving and restoring art

B. Digitizing works of art

C. Protecting art in conflict zones

D. All of the above

13. In European art, why was the Renaissance period important?

A. Because you can't just jump right from Medieval art to Abstract art without confusing people

B. It marked a revival of classical ideas and techniques, leading to a surge in scientific exploration and artistic achievement

C. Because the pope said so

D. It's the prettiest artwork ever

14. What is one example of Eastern European art?

A. Samurai swords

B. Hula dancing

C. Flamenco dresses

D. Icon painting

15. What is one of the important movements in Asian art?

    A. Japan's Ukiyo-e

    B. The art of making sushi

    C. The art of Thai massage

    D. The art of Vietnamese flower markets

16. In Pacific Islander art, what is tapa cloth?

    A. The fabric your hulu skirt is made from

    B. What they put under your tapas in Spain

    C. A type of bark cloth made from the inner bark of trees, which is then beaten and painted with intricate designs

    D. Not sure but it sounds important

17. Who was Frida Kahlo?

A. The first CEO of Fendi

B. A Mexican artist who painted deeply personal and emotive self portraits

C. The owner of Frito Lay

D. A magical princess in a fairytale

18. What are some examples of Mayan art?

A. That awesome hot chocolate you had last year

B. Intricate jade carvings, ornate pottery, and magnificent stone monuments depicting gods and rulers

C. Fabulous earrings that Beyoncé might wear

D. A 1000-piece sundial jigsaw puzzle

19. Who is **Roberto Matta from Chile?**

    A. An influential surrealist artist whose works explore the depths of the subconscious and cosmic themes

    B. An art teacher at your university

    C. A chef at the new Michelin Star restaurant in London

    D. The dance teacher who taught Fred Astaire how to dance

20. Why are the **terracotta sculptures of the Nok culture in Nigeria so important?**

    A. They are really heavy

    B. They made sculptures depict human figures with elaborate hairstyles, intricate jewelry, and facial scarification, providing insights into the social and cultural life of ancient African societies

    C. You can only buy them through an app

    D. Because they are collector's items

21. Why is Islamic calligraphy so important?

A. It showcases the mastery of skilled calligraphers who transform Arabic script into elegant and intricate designs

B. Because no one knows how to write in cursive anymore

C. It's the only way to understand ancient poetry

D. It's a direct translation of beautiful music and dance

22. What is AR art?

A. Augmented Reality (AR) is the art you make after you've had a few too many drinks at the club

B. Augmented Reality (AR) is art you don't understand

C. Augmented Reality (AR) is an integration of digital content onto the physical world

D. Augmented Reality (AR) is art in science fiction movies

23. What can VR help us do in the arts and culture world?

A. Virtual Reality (VR) art is like when I ask Siri for the answer to "what is virtual reality?"

B. Virtual Reality (VR) is the art of trying on clothes online after I take a cute selfie to upload on the store's site

C. Virtual Reality (VR) requires you to hold your breath while you look at underwater art

D. Virtual Reality (VR) artists harness the full potential of three-dimensional space to craft mesmerizing masterpieces

24. Who is Banksy?

A. The guy who runs banks

B. Someone with a fancy accent

C. An anonymous and elusive street artist

D. A James Bond villain

25. What are NFTs?

A. Non-Fungible Tokens are digital certificates of authenticity, immutably recorded on blockchain technology

B. Not Fun Time like when you don't like a concert

C. Never Finding the Truth is what happens when you look at abstract art

D. Nice Fancy T-shirts are what you wear to a music festival

26. What is interactive art?

A. When a child acts out at the museum

B. Artistic experiences that transcend the norms and engage both humans and machines

C. Artwork that has a musical soundtrack

D. When I get to touch the sculpture

27. What is art therapy?

   A. A therapeutic approach that utilizes the creative process of art-making to foster emotional, psychological, and mental well-being

   B. What I need when I've done too many drawings and my hands cramp up

   C. When the service dog makes a painted paw print on paper

   D. When you make a film about crystals and yoga

28. What is one example of the Science + Art movement?

   A. When the doctor wears colorful scrubs

   B. The board game Pictionary

   C. When they make the pastries super pretty at the French Patisseries

   D. The Bioluminescent Night Walk project by the American Museum of Natural History

29. Who holds the record for the largest film output annually?

    A. Toronto Film School

    B. Bollywood

    C. Disney

    D. Clint Eastwood

30. Why is it controversial to invest in art as a commodity?

    A. Because art is not a real investment, it's just a bunch of pretty pictures

    B. Because art is only valuable if it's made by a famous artist, and those artists are all dead

    C. Because art is a risky investment, and you could lose all your money if you don't know what you're doing

    D. Because some artworks are seen more as financial assets than expressions of creativity and culture

31. What language is Opera in?

A. The language of love

B. Opera is in a language that is made up of random sounds that sound good together

C. The language they were composed in, such as Italian, German, French, or English, depending on the production

D. Opera is in a language that only opera singers can understand

32. What is abstract art?

A. Art that is made by people who are too lazy to draw anything real

B. Art that is only valuable if it is made by someone who is really good at math

C. A style of visual art that does not attempt to represent an accurate depiction of visual reality

D. Art that is only valuable if it can be used as a Rorschach test

33. What is blue chip art?

A. Artworks by highly esteemed and established artists that have gained significant recognition, value, and market demand

B. A type of art that is made with blue paint

C. A type of art that is only valuable if it is blue

D. A type of art that is only valuable if it is made by a blue-haired artist

34. What is chiaroscuro?

A. A type of Italian pasta that is made with dark and light noodles

B. A technique used in visual arts, particularly in painting, to create a strong contrast between light and dark

C. A type of dance that is performed in the dark

D. A type of martial art that uses light and dark energy to fight

35. What is **crypto** art?

    A. It's art from the **crypts** of ancient **Egypt**

    B. It's what **scammers** do when they upload a pirated painting online

    C. Artwork for people who want to show off how much money they have

    D. Digital **art**works that are **cr**eated, **bou**ght, sold, and owned using blockchain technology and cryptocurrencies

36. What is an art **re**view?

    A. An art review is a long-winded way of saying "I didn't like it."

    B. A report card for movies, books, music, art shows

    C. A way to show off your vocabulary without actually saying anything

    D. A way to justify spending a lot of money on something you don't understand

37. What is a triptych?

A. A painting that's really hard to fold up

B. A composition that consists of three separate panels or sections that are displayed together as a single artwork

C. A painting that's three times as good as a diptych

D. A painting that's always on sale at IKEA

38. What is the difference between an art gallery and a museum?

A. An art gallery is a space dedicated to exhibiting and showcasing visual art. A museum is a space dedicated to the collection, preservation, exhibition, and interpretation of objects or artworks that have historical, cultural, scientific, or artistic significance.

B. Art galleries serve champagne while museums serve martinis

C. Art galleries are in NYC hipster neighborhoods and museums are in big buildings in ancient cities

D. Art galleries require a formal dress code and museums require that you buy those audio headset things

39. Name one famous art fair.

    A. Euro Disney

    B. Art Basel Miami Beach

    C. The Ritz Carlton

    D. Starbucks

40. What can you expect at a poetry reading?

    A. One can expect to be immersed in a world of lyrical beauty and emotional resonance

    B. One can expect an open bar

    C. One can expect to dress up in superhero costumes

    D. One can expect to rhyme on time for a dime with a chime while eating a lime

41. Name **a famous film fest**ival?

    A. Movie **night at your gran**dma's **hou**se

    B. The opening **night of any Tom Cru**ise **act**ion **movie**

    C. A Lord of the Rings **mara**thon

    D. Cannes **Film Fest**ival

42. **The m**ost **famous Oktobe**rfest **is hel**d **in whi**ch **ci**ty?

    A. Windhoek

    B. Vancouver

    C. Munich

    D. Santiago

43. Some careers in Arts and Culture Management include what?

    A. Event manager

    B. Marketing and promotion manager

    C. Fundraising manager

    D. All of the above

44. What skills do glassblowers need?

    A. They must be skilled in both tough love and critical thinking

    B. They must be skilled in both hand-eye coordination and precision

    C. They must be skilled in both combat arms and judo

    D. They must be skilled in both dog whispering and cat sitting

45. What is **Winterlude**?

> **A. A celebration of winter featuring a variety of activities, including skating, snowshoeing, ice carving, and concerts**

> **B. A section of Disneyland where you dress up in puffy coats and eat ice cream**

> **C. When you forget to turn your air conditioner off**

> **D. The holiday between fall semester and spring semester**

46. How **would you dress for an art auction**?

> **A. The dress code for an art auction is typically formal or semi-formal**

> **B. The dress code for an art auction is anything goes**

> **C. The dress code for an art auction is typically jeans and a T-shirt**

> **D. The dress code for an art auction is Gucci only**

47. Why would you go to a writer's retreat?

   A. To learn how to rhyme

   B. Because you failed English class

   C. Writer's retreats allow writers to connect with each other, share ideas, and learn from one another

   D. Writer's retreats are for really stressed-out graduate students trying to write their thesis

48. What is the purpose of a sound bath?

   A. They are a way to wash all the loud noises out of your ears after a concert

   B. They are a way to way to reduce stress, improve your sleep, or simply relax

   C. They are a good way for people to chill out before they get their ears pierced

   D. They are a way to discover a new Spotify playlist

49. What are some of the principles of Burning Man?

    A. Radical Inclusion

    B. Communal Effort

    C. Participation

    D. All of the above

50. Why is recycled art important?

    A. It helps me understand the number inside the triangle arrows on the bottom of your plastic containers

    B. It provides a new way to create art that is both beautiful and environmentally friendly

    C. Because nobody likes litterbugs

    D. Because we're all out of fresh ideas for art

CHAPTER 8 ✿ Pssst- Check Yourself

You want answers? You want the truth? You CAN handle the truth!

~

1. **D.** The arts are for everyone because they do all these things and more! The arts also cultivate creativity, nurture mental well-being, embody cultural heritage, inspire resilience and adaptability, enhance aesthetics in design and innovation, catalyze personal growth, and fuel a lifelong love for learning. Go art!

2. **A.** The arts, with their myriad forms and manifestations, play a pivotal role in celebrating and promoting diversity. They act as catalysts for cultural progression, welcoming freedom of expression, fostering empathy, appreciating minority artists, resurrecting forgotten art, and encouraging us to embrace our differences.

3. **B.** The Dawn of Art - From Cave Walls to Timeless Treasures: Our artistic voyage begins in prehistoric times, when our ancestors, adorned with creativity, left their mark on cave walls with vivid paintings and handprints. These early artworks, dating back over 40,000 years, were a testament to the human desire to express their world, spirituality, and connection with nature.

4. **C.** The Digital Art Revolution: Digital art, already a driving force in contemporary art, will continue to expand its frontiers. Advancements in virtual and

augmented reality will immerse viewers in interactive art experiences, blurring the boundaries between the real and the virtual. Artists will harness the potential of AI and machine learning to create artworks that respond and adapt to viewers' emotions and reactions, creating personalized artistic encounters.

5. D. Space Art Exploration: As humanity ventures further into space, art will accompany this cosmic odyssey. Space artists will capture the celestial wonders and challenges of interplanetary exploration, inspiring us to contemplate our place in the cosmos and the boundaries of human endeavor. Experiments will also produce new art techniques, because someday we'll be writing this from Mars, and we're not sure if we can type so well with those big astronaut gloves on...

6. A. Bioart and Sustainability: Artists will increasingly engage with biotechnology, exploring the convergence of art and science. Bioart will raise profound ethical and environmental questions while highlighting the urgency of sustainability. The fusion of living organisms and artistic expression will challenge our perception of art's boundaries.

7. D. Neuroart and Mindscapes: The exploration of brain-computer interfaces and neurotechnology will lead to the emergence of neuroart. Artists will create mind-bending art experiences that interface with the viewer's neural activity, pushing the boundaries of consciousness and perception.

8. **A**. Religion - The **Symp**hony of **Spirit**uality: **Religi**ous **beliefs, a source of prof**ound **inspira**tion **for many, find expre**ssion **through cult**ural **rituals and traditions. The**se **age-ol**d **practices enrich our lives, envel**oping **us in the harm**ony **of spiritual expre**ssion. From **color**ful **festi**vals to awe-**inspir**ing **ceremo**nies, **cult**ure **channels the divine in a way that unites hea**rts and **celeb**rates our **shared spirit**ual **jour**ney.

9. **A. Freep**orts - The Secret **Va**ults **of Treas**ures: **Conce**aled **within bust**ling **cities or nest**led **disc**reetly **near airports, freeports are enigm**atic **sanctu**aries **that house the world's most valu**able **cultural treasures. The**se **high-security faci**lities **remain veiled in secrecy, holding count**less **master**pieces **and rare artif**acts. The **labyrin**thine **halls of freeports, with their temperature- controlled vaults and impene**trable **security, have beco**me **the stage for thril**ling **spy novels and Holly**wood **blockb**usters. We **can't help but imag**ine **the mysteries that lie behind tho**se **guar**ded **doo**rs. **C**an **you say "tax haven"?**

10. **D. Cul**tural **Repat**riation - **A Que**st for Lost **Heri**tage: The **que**st to **repat**riate **cult**ural **treasures to their countries of origin is a sto**ry of **moral conscience and global collabo**ration. As **ancient artifacts find their way back home after years of being housed in foreign collec**tions, **these heartw**arming **stories embody the triu**mph **of cultural heritage and unity. Countries and institutions world**wide **work toge**ther **to return these cultural icons, a reminder of the glo**bal **effort to preserve our shared past.**

11. C. Cultural Heritage at Risk - A Race Against Time: As the world undergoes transformation, the fate of cultural heritage hangs in the balance. Climate change, urbanization, and conflict pose existential threats to countless cultural landmarks. Stories of preservation and restoration efforts in the face of these challenges capture our attention, inspiring us to cherish and safeguard our artistic heritage. Efforts to preserve endangered monuments, ancient ruins, and cultural landmarks serve as poignant reminders of our shared responsibility to protect and cherish our cultural legacy.

12. D. Cultural archaeologists (that's all of us, friends) try to safeguard our cultural heritage and ensure its passage to future generations. Some ways of doing this are: preservation through conservation, digitization, protecting cultural heritage sites, protecting art in conflict zones, preparing for emergency response for art, community engagement, cross-cultural collaboration, protecting street art, and education and advocacy.

13. B. Movements in the European art world have played a significant role in shaping the direction of artistic expression. The Renaissance period, for example, marked a revival of classical ideas and techniques, leading to a surge in scientific exploration and artistic achievements.

14. D. One of the standout art forms in Eastern European art is icon painting. Rooted in the Byzantine tradition, iconography holds a

significant place in the religious and cultural life of Eastern European communities. Icons are religious images, typically painted on wood panels, and are characterized by their flat, symbolic style and richly detailed ornamentation. These religious artworks serve as a means of spiritual devotion, storytelling, and cultural identity.

15. **A**. One important movement in Asian art is the Ukiyo-e in Japan, which flourished during the Edo period. Ukiyo-e prints were made using woodblock techniques and were often mass-produced, making art accessible to a broader audience. These prints showcased scenes from daily life, kabuki actors, and beautiful landscapes, capturing the essence of Japanese culture during that time.

16. **C**. One of the standout art forms in Pacific Islander art is the mesmerizing tapa cloth. This is a type of bark cloth made from the inner bark of trees, which is then beaten and painted with intricate designs. Tapa cloths often tell stories, depict important events, or showcase traditional motifs that reflect the cultural identity of the Pacific Island communities.

17. **B**. One name that should ring a bell is Frida Kahlo, a Mexican artist who lived and worked in the early 20th century. Kahlo's deeply personal and emotive self-portraits, often featuring symbolic elements and surrealistic touches, have made her an icon of self-expression and feminism.

18. **B.** The ancient Maya civilization, for example, left behind a legacy of stunning artwork, including intricate jade carvings, ornate pottery, and magnificent stone monuments depicting gods and rulers. Their art reflects their deep connection to nature, their complex cosmology, and their impressive artistic skills.

19. **A.** Another notable figure is Roberto Matta from Chile, an influential surrealist artist whose works explore the depths of the subconscious and cosmic themes.

20. **B.** When it comes to famous artworks in African art, one that deserves mention is the exquisite terracotta sculptures of the Nok culture in Nigeria. Dating back over 2,000 years, these sculptures depict human figures with elaborate hairstyles, intricate jewelry, and facial scarification, providing insights into the social and cultural life of ancient African societies.

21. **A.** When exploring Middle Eastern art history, it is impossible not to mention the mesmerizing beauty of Islamic calligraphy. Calligraphy, often revered as the highest art form in the Islamic world, showcases the mastery of skilled calligraphers who transform Arabic script into elegant and intricate designs. These sacred writings, found in religious texts, architectural elements, and artworks, serve as a visual representation of spirituality and devotion.

22. **C.** Augmented Reality (AR) is an integration of digital content onto the physical world. Artists

utilize AR apps or devices like smartphones and tablets to create interactive experiences that blur the line between the real and the virtual.

23. **D.** Virtual Reality (VR) offers an **unparalleled** immersive experience, transporting users to computer-generated environments through VR headsets like Oculus Rift or HTC Vive. In the realm of VR art, artists harness the full potential of three-dimensional space to craft mesmerizing masterpieces. Platforms like Google Tilt Brush provide artists with a virtual canvas to create intricate and breathtaking works of art. Additionally, attendees can virtually witness live performances by their favorite musicians from the front row through apps like MelodyVR, revolutionizing the concert experience.

24. **C.** The anonymous identity of the elusive street artist Banksy has become one of the most enduring art mysteries of our time, shrouding the artist's persona in an air of mystique.

25. **A.** Enter the world of Non-Fungible Tokens (NFTs), the magic behind the uniqueness of Online Art. NFTs are digital certificates of authenticity, immutably recorded on blockchain technology. They grant ownership and prove the rarity of a specific digital creation, whether it be a digital painting, a GIF, or a virtual sculpture. With NFTs, artists can forever imbue their digital works with uniqueness, and collectors can truly own a piece of the digital marvel.

26. **B.** In the **mesmer**izing **world** of **inter**active art, artistic **experi**ences **trans**cend the **norms** and **eng**age **both hum**ans and **mach**ines. **Intera**ctive **art installa**tions **have ushe**red **in a para**digm **shi**ft, **offer**ing **arti**sts and **audie**nces **a dyna**mic **dial**ogue that **leads** to **both wins** and **los**ses. **Wins** in **inter**active **art lie in the pro**found **level of engag**ement and **immer**sion it **fost**ers. **By brea**king **down the barriers betwe**en **arti**sts and **audie**nces, **inter**active **art blurs the lines of autho**rship and **inv**ites **ever**yone **to be a parti**cipant, **co-crea**ting the **experi**ence. **This fost**ers **a sen**se of **owner**ship, **mak**ing the **artwork deeply pers**onal and **emotio**nally **reso**nant. **Intera**ctive **installa**tions **beco**me **memora**ble, **leav**ing **a lasti**ng **imp**act **on vis**itors, **foste**ring **mean**ingful **connec**tions, and **broad**ening the **app**eal of **contem**porary art.

27. **A.** Art **therapy** is **a therap**eutic **appr**oach that **util**izes the **crea**tive **proce**ss of art-**mak**ing to **fos**ter **emot**ional, **psychol**ogical, and **ment**al **well-being. It prov**ides **a safe** and **expre**ssive **out**let for **indiv**iduals **to commun**icate, **expl**ore, and **under**stand **their emot**ions, **thou**ghts, and **experi**ences **thro**ugh art. **Unl**ike **tradit**ional **talk ther**apy, art **ther**apy **eng**ages the **crea**tive **right hemis**phere **of the brain, allo**wing for **deep**er self-**explor**ation and **heal**ing.

28. **D.** These **proj**ects can **take many differ**ent forms, from **inter**active **installa**tions to **perfor**mance art to **public** art. For **exam**ple, the **Biolumi**nescent **Night Walk proj**ect by the **Ameri**can **Mus**eum of **Nat**ural **Hist**ory **uses biolumi**nescent **bac**teria to

create a magical nighttime experience. Visitors can walk through a forest of glowing trees and plants, and they can even learn about the science behind bioluminescence.

29. **B. Boasting over 1,000 films produced annually, Bollywood holds the record for the largest film output globally. Stepping back to 1913, we witness the birth of Indian cinema with the premiere of "Raja Harishchandra," a pioneering moment that laid the foundation for Bollywood's illustrious storytelling tradition.**

30. **D. Art as Investment or Commodity: As art values escalate, the perception of art as a lucrative investment opportunity has grown. This has led to the commodification of art, where some artworks are seen more as financial assets than expressions of creativity and culture. The commercialization of art has sparked debates about its impact on artistic integrity and the exclusion of aspiring artists from the market.**

31. **C. Language: Operas are typically performed in the language they were composed in, such as Italian, German, French, or English, depending on the production. However, most opera houses provide supertitles or subtitles projected above the stage or on individual screens, translating the lyrics into the language of the audience. This allows you to follow the storyline and understand the dialogue even if you're not familiar with the language.**

32. **C**. Abstract art is a style of visual art that does not attempt to represent an accurate depiction of visual reality. Instead, it uses shapes, colors, forms, and marks to achieve its effect. In abstract art, the artist may choose to focus on the expressive qualities of the artwork rather than its representational aspects. This style of art often emphasizes the emotional or spiritual dimensions of the artist's experience, allowing for an interpretation up to the viewer.

33. **A**. Blue chip art refers to artworks by highly esteemed and established artists that have gained significant recognition, value, and market demand. It's like the top-tier, highly sought-after artworks that are considered prestigious within the art world.

34. **B**. Chiaroscuro is a technique used in visual arts, particularly in painting, to create a strong contrast between light and dark. It involves the skillful use of light and shadow to give depth and volume to a composition. The term "chiaroscuro" comes from the Italian words "chiaro" meaning light and "scuro" meaning dark. This technique has been used by artists throughout history to create dramatic and realistic effects in their artwork.

35. **D**. Crypto art refers to digital artworks that are created, bought, sold, and owned using blockchain technology and cryptocurrencies. It's a new frontier where technology and art intersect, allowing artists to create, share, and monetize their digital creations in unique and innovative ways.

36. **C.** In the arts and culture world, a review is a report card for movies, books, music, art shows. It shares a critic's thoughts and feelings about that creative masterpiece. Reviews help you decide what to check out or avoid, just like a compass guiding you to the coolest artworks and cultural events, or steering you away from not-so-great ones.

37. **B.** Triptych is a composition that consists of three separate panels or sections that are displayed together as a single artwork. It's a storytelling format where each panel contributes to a larger narrative or visual exploration. Triptychs have been used throughout history and across various artistic mediums, including painting, photography, and digital art.

38. **A.** An art gallery is a space dedicated to exhibiting and showcasing visual art, including paintings, sculptures, photographs, installations, and more. It is a venue for artists to present their work to the public and for visitors to engage with and appreciate various forms of artistic expression. Galleries are free to enter, and the gallerists love to talk with visitors about the artists represented and the artworks on display ... A museum is a space dedicated to the collection, preservation, exhibition, and interpretation of objects or artworks that have historical, cultural, scientific, or artistic significance. Museums can house a wide range of exhibits, including artifacts, paintings, sculptures, photographs, interactive displays, and more. They provide an opportunity to explore and learn about various

subjects and aspects of human history and creativity.

39. **B.** Here are the top 10 art fairs in the world: Art Basel Miami Beach, Frieze London, Art Basel Hong Kong, The Armory Show, Artissima, FIAC, SCOPE, VOLTA New York, Scope Basel, The Other Art Fair.

40. **A.** When attending a poetry reading, one can expect to be immersed in a world of lyrical beauty and emotional resonance. The atmosphere is often intimate, with a strong sense of camaraderie and appreciation for the art of poetry.

41. **D.** Some of the most well-known film festivals include the Cannes Film Festival, the Sundance Film Festival, and the Toronto International Film Festival. These events are renowned for their exceptional programming, world-class films, and unparalleled atmosphere.

42. **C.** Oktoberfest is the world's largest Volksfest (beer festival) and is held annually in Munich, Bavaria, Germany. It is a 16-day event running from late September to the first weekend in October where you can party with more than six million of your closest friends from around the world.

43. **D.** Some careers in arts and cultural event management include: // Event manager: Event managers are responsible for the overall planning, organization, and execution of events.

They work with a variety of stakeholders to ensure that events run smoothly and that guests have a memorable experience. // Venue manager: Venue managers are responsible for the day-to-day operations of a venue, such as a theater, concert hall, or museum. They oversee the booking of events, the maintenance of the facility, and the staff. // Marketing and promotion manager: Marketing and promotion managers are responsible for creating and executing marketing campaigns for events. They work to generate awareness of events and to encourage people to attend. // Fundraising manager: Fundraising managers are responsible for raising money to support arts and cultural events. They work with donors to secure funding and to manage the finances of events.

44. B. Glassblowing is a centuries-old art form that involves shaping molten glass into objects of beauty and utility. It is a hot and dangerous process, but it can also be incredibly rewarding. Glassblowers use a variety of tools and techniques to create their work, including blowpipes, shears, and paddles. They must be skilled in both hand-eye coordination and precision.

45. A. Winterlude is an annual winter festival held in Ottawa, Canada. It is a celebration of winter featuring a variety of activities, including skating, snowshoeing, ice carving, and concerts. This jam is cool because you've got art, winter sports, and activities.

46. **A**. The **dress code** for an art **auction** is **typic**ally **formal** or **semi-formal**, as it is a high-end **event**. **Some** of the **most famous** art **auct**ions **inclu**de the **Christie's** and **Sotheby's auctions**, **which** are **kno**wn for **selling some** of the **most expen**sive **artwork** in the **world**. At an art **auc**tion, you **can expect** to see a **vari**ety of **peo**ple, **inclu**ding **collec**tors, art **enthus**iasts, and **weal**thy **individ**uals. They **will** be **bidd**ing on **artwork** and **discu**ssing the **pie**ces with **each other**.

47. **C**. **A writer's retr**eat is a **gath**ering of **writ**ers who **come tog**ether to **work** on **their cra**ft in a **suppo**rtive and **inspi**ring **enviro**nment. It's an **impo**rtant **part** of the **arts** and **culture world becau**se it **allows writ**ers to **conn**ect with **each other**, **share ideas**, and **learn** from one **ano**ther.

48. **B**. **Sou**nd **baths** can be a **very rela**xing and **bene**ficial **experi**ence. **If** you are **look**ing for a **way** to **red**uce **stress**, **impr**ove **your sle**ep, or **sim**ply **rel**ax, **defini**tely **try** a **sou**nd **bath**.

49. **D**. There are 10 **princ**iples of **Burn**ing **Man**: **Rad**ical **Inc**lusion, **Gift**ing, **Decommod**ification, **Radical Self-reli**ance, **Radical Self-expre**ssion, **Comm**unal **Effort**, **Civic Respons**ibility, **Leav**ing **No Tra**ce, **Partici**pation, and **Immed**iacy.

50. **B**. **This** is a **grow**ing **trend** that is **mak**ing a **posi**tive **imp**act on the **enviro**nment and the **arts**. **It prov**ides a **new way** to **cre**ate art that is **bo**th **beaut**iful and **environm**entally **fri**endly. **It insp**ires **peo**ple to **think ab**out the **environ**ment and how **they** can **red**uce **their imp**act on the **pl**anet. **It's** a

276

unique and creative way to express oneself, and it is a powerful way to raise awareness of waste, recycling, and environmental issues.

Acknowledgments ❀ Because saying "Thank You" is super polite.

~

Our global colleagues in Rome were the bomb. They dropped mad knowledge on the arts, culture, and art history. Our advisor, Professor Alexandra Solea, and the rest of the Rome Business School crew were always down to answer our burning questions, even the most scandalous ones. We learned a lot, and now we're officially cool.

But you know who's cooler than us? Our life partners. They put up with us spouting off rad art facts all the time while we created this beast of an art book. You'd love them as much as we do.

Biography of the three badasses who created this gem:

In the rapidly evolving world of art, culture, and social transformation, these three extraordinary individuals stand as beacons of inspiration for Generations Y and Z. Nechama Hermon, Ashley Ludwig, and Dr. Bethany Miller have joined forces to ignite a movement that blends their diverse expertise, experiences, and passion. Together, they form the powerhouse trio of cultural catalysts.

They are unleashing creativity, connection, and change.

~

Nechama Hermon, an Arts & Culture specialist hailing from Austria, is an art historian with an unwavering commitment to preserving cultural heritage. Her extensive knowledge of Jewish history, multicultural traditions, and international arts has taken her across Europe. Having worked in prestigious auction houses, museums, and restoration studios, Nechama's unique strength lies in her ability to share a visionary perspective that transcends boundaries.

~

From Italy comes Ashley Ludwig, the executive coordinator who fuses her expertise in psychology, mental wellbeing, and creative community planning with her passion for the arts. With a remarkable track record in events, public relations, and educational management, Ashley has collaborated with top-level executives to drive transformational training and foster cultural and social change. Her exceptional strength lies in her boundless creativity, which fuels her commitment to building inclusive and vibrant communities.

~

Completing this dynamic trio is Dr. Bethany Miller, a seasoned consultant and coach based in the United States but living nomadically. With a Ph.D. and a diverse background in management, logistics, aviation, and the arts, Bethany's expertise spans multiple sectors. After a successful career as a pilot, she transitioned into advising and project development, leveraging her exceptional organizational skills to bring structure and efficiency to the world of arts and cultural projects. Bethany's strength lies in her ability to orchestrate complex endeavors with precision and finesse.

~

In their collective pursuit, Nechama, Ashley, and Bethany are rewriting the rulebook on how cultural initiatives can shape our society. Through their collaborative efforts, they aim to unleash creativity, foster connection, and ignite transformative change. Their book serves as a manifesto for Generations Y and Z, inviting them to embrace the power of art, culture, and community as catalysts for a better future.

~